# ALPHABETS
# FOR ENGLISH

The series of volumes,
of which this is the first,
is inscribed to the memory of
Dr. Mont Follick.

MONT FOLLICK SERIES
VOLUME 1

# ALPHABETS FOR ENGLISH

*edited by*
W. HAAS

MANCHESTER
UNIVERSITY PRESS

MANCHESTER UNIVERSITY PRESS
316–324 Oxford Road
Manchester M13 9NR, England

GB SBN 7190 0391 1

PE
1150
H23

Printed in Great Britain by The Pitman Press, Bath

# Contents

# Note

The lectures on which these chapters are based were given under the auspices of the Mont Follick Trust in the University of Manchester.

Chapter 2, Sir James Pitman's on 7 February 1964
Chapter 3, Dr. Axel Wijk's on 28 January 1965
Chapter 4, P. A. D. MacCarthy's on 16 March 1965
Chapter 5, P. A. D. MacCarthy's on 18 November 1966

# 1

## On 'Spelling'
## and 'Spelling Reform'

*by*
W. Haas

THE studies contained in this volume occupy themselves with familiar matters. What is generally taken for granted, is here subjected to critical scrutiny—not always an easy task, but sometimes a surprisingly rewarding one.

Elementary education enables us, by a mere process of habit-formation and without much expense of thought, to acquire some of the basic achievements of our civilization. We 'learn the figures' without marvelling at the efficiency of the 'Arabic' notation (which, had he but come upon it, would have given supreme delight to any Roman geometer or trader); and we learn to read and write without recognizing the enormous achievement of the alphabet. It is true that the 'thoughtlessness', with which we now acquire and use those gifts from a distant past, has its advantage: it permits us to learn it all very early and to save our thought for other things. But such semi-automatic inheritance can be a drawback. Flaws may begin to develop in the equipment which is passed on as a fixed social institution; and without clearer awareness of its working structure and significance, we should hardly be able to deal with its defects.

1

The art of writing is one of the ancient arts and crafts in which the science of language has its origin. It is among the oldest of them, obviously reaching back as far as the beginnings of recorded history. Since then, the development of linguistics has continued to yield further technological advances: dictionaries and grammars of hundreds of languages, methods of language-teaching, notations for a variety of purposes, from logic and mathematics to shorthand and computer programming. But among these advances and, indeed, among all the gadgets of our modern age, the most ancient achievement—the art of writing, and especially alphabetic writing—remains unsurpassed in importance to the present day. As human civilization could not even begin to develop without this art, so a training in it remains the first step—the inevitable first step—for every child entering upon his cultural heritage.

Of all intellectual traditions, none are more firmly established than those which are passed on to little children in their first years of school. Such traditions tend to continue unchanged—safe from argument, and inaccessible to criticism. This is their power as well as their weakness. We never think of them. We are too young to do so when we learn them; and having learned them, we are loath to expend thought on what by then is a mechanical skill. We are glad, at last, to be able to think of *what* we read or write, without being distracted by problems of how to do it. No wonder, then, that we are instinctively protective about our mechanical skills. But to protect a mechanical skill is, precisely, to avoid thinking about it. For thought about it threatens all the advantage it has of saving thought for something else.

This explains why the mere sight of a new alphabet is enough to deter many who would like to learn Russian from even making a start. Proposals for spelling reform arouse a similar instinctively defensive opposition. Such violent reactions are not quite so irrational as they are sometimes made out to be. True, the task of memorizing a new set of letters is easy enough. Once the art of reading has been acquired through one set of symbols, it takes very little time and effort to 'know' the use of another. But 'knowing' is only the first step; for we have not learned a new alphabet, until we have made our use of it as 'thoughtless' and mechanical as the use of the old one had been. And this takes time. It is because of the difficulty of replacing it, that we are always ready to defend a semi-automatic habit. We do not relish the prospect of becoming spelling toddlers once more.

And yet, it would be a pity, if all the knowledge people have of this supreme tool of human civilization were to remain for ever at a toddler's level. Indeed, we might succeed, some day, in raising even this level, if we can bring ourselves to see in 'spelling' something more than the dead letter of tradition.

Attempts are being made at present to enliven the teaching of arithmetic in our schools. Mechanical exercises are to be replaced, or at least supplemented, by mathematical explorations. The children are to do arithmetic as an answer to questions they have first learned to ask. It is not impossible that, some day, the teaching of writing will be enlivened in a similar way.

At present, however, among those who have acquired the art, there are surely not very many who know of the discovery which made it possible. And yet, it was a sensational discovery. When Plato wished to illustrate the power and techniques of scientific analysis, he was fond of referring to this marvellous reduction of all speech to just a few 'letters'. The facts which are the foundation of alphabetic writing must have been unexpected as well as hidden. How else could we explain that, in the long history of the human race, the alphabet appears to have been discovered only once—by a Near-Eastern people speaking a Semitic language? All the alphabets we know appear to be descended from this one source.

That the practically infinite number of different utterances which may be produced and understood in a community should be capable of being reduced to a limited number of 'units of meaning' (ideas, words, roots)—this has occurred

3

to many. Significant elements, however, such as words, must still be counted in thousands. No efficient technique of writing could be based on assigning thousands of different symbols to the thousands of lexical elements. In a society operating with such a convention (as the Chinese still do), it is obviously very difficult for all its members to become literate; the task is too hard, and too time-consuming.

The idea that analysis of utterances could be pushed further—that is, beyond identifying significant units—to yield smaller recurrent elements which, though *constituting* significant utterances, may themselves *have no meaning at all* —this idea cannot have been easy to come by. And the result of such analysis ('phonological analysis') was truly surprising: the practically infinite number of different utterances turned out to be capable of reduction to just a few dozens of recurring 'sounds'. Now, and only now, was it possible to represent any of that unlimited number with the help of just a few dozen signs; and also possible, at once, to spread scholarship from a few priests and clerks to the people, and to develop that kind of modern society which relies on the literacy of its members.

This is a great story; one can understand Plato's fondness for it. But among all the children in our schools, and among the adults who have learned to read and write when they were children, how many have ever experienced anything of the wonder and surprise which rewarded the discoverers and designers of their alphabet? Most of us have never learned to ask the questions to which our alphabet is an answer. And having never looked at it as being the solution of an analytic and technological problem, most of us, its users, never ask, *how adequate* a solution it is. And yet, such questions are obviously nothing less than a concern with the technological foundations of our society and civilization. And they happen to be of special urgency for readers and writers of English.

4

English orthography, as we all know, has long ceased to make proper use of the advantages of alphabetic writing. This is of course not due to any deep irrational strain in the English character. As in the case of most irrational institutions, there is an historical explanation. When, about 500 years ago, English spelling became conventionally fixed in more or less its present shape, the spoken language was yet to undergo extensive changes. As a result of these changes, the same letter would come to represent a number of different sounds (e.g. the letter 'a' in *same, fat, call, fast*), or indeed no sound at all (as the 'silent letters' in *know* or *wrestle*). But since at that time reading and writing was only the privilege of certain leisured classes, the inconsistency of English spelling was not felt to be any special disadvantage. On the contrary, its anecdotal archaic flavour was sufficiently appreciated to discourage ideas of reform. It was enjoyable to discover in one's script some fossils of an earlier age. Also, to be able to spell correctly came to be a welcome sign of 'class', and of more than average education. Inconsistency, however, if not removed, continues to breed further inconsistency. An esoteric concern with etymologies and pseudo-etymologies, rather than any regard for an efficient script, went on moulding English spelling conventions for centuries. It was only after the arrival of general education that the drawbacks of the archaic script were felt to be serious. Not every reader and writer of English could now be expected to know French and Latin; and there would be few, even among the educated, to appreciate that exquisite game of computing English spelling from a historical knowledge of three languages.

It should be admitted that present English orthography is not without interest, that it even has some advantages. The 'irregular' spelling of thousands of loan-words and technical terms is close to the spelling of similar words in other European languages—much closer than a phonetic English spelling would be. A Frenchman or German, who cannot understand a single sentence of spoken English, may yet find it fairly easy to grasp the substance of an English scientific text by silent reading. He would find it more difficult, if the script were faithful to that English speech which he cannot follow. Even for the English user, the phonetically deviant orthography provides some useful non-phonetic signals. For example, there is a certain advantage in marking the English plural always by *s* (though the phonetic value is either /s/ or /z/), or marking the English preterite always by *d* (instead of writing for it, in phonetically faithful fashion, sometimes /d/ and sometimes /t/). Again, there is some sense in distinguishing the phonetically identical final vowels /ə/ of 'polar', 'author', 'baker', so as to relate them to 'polarity', 'authority' and 'bakery', respectively.[1] It is important to remember in this connection that a *writing system*, even of the alphabetic sort, is never simply a phonetic transcription. Some of its deviations from a phonetic script—such as those just mentioned—are well motivated even from a purely linguistic point of view.[2]

However, even if we do not subscribe to any wholesale condemnation of English orthography, or to the idea that a perfect phonetic script would be best for English, it still seems impossible to deny that, on the whole, English-speaking communities are paying a heavy price for their analphabetic traditions. Their school-children have to waste a great deal of time learning an unnecessarily difficult technique of reading and writing; and there is continual waste of time and of material resources in writing and printing superfluous letters. These are serious drawbacks, and not only for the English speaking communities. For, in the same way, the use of English as a second language is being obstructed in all parts of the world.

It is on account of these social consequences that English

1. It is remarkable that Sir James Pitman accepts the phonetically deviant representations of [ə] (*Learning to Read, p.* 19), while rejecting plural -*s* and preterite -*d*.

2. Cf. Josef Vachek, *Some remarks on writing and phonetic transcription* (in 'Readings in Linguistics, ii', University of Chicago Press, 1966).

spelling traditions have come under attack from many quarters—from teachers, writers, and politicians no less than students of language: from teachers, who feel in duty bound to voice the pains of their spelling infants; from writers, reflecting on the inefficiency of their tools; and from politicians, concerned about the educational level of their fellow-citizens, or about obstacles to the international use of English. Dr. Follick, teacher and politician, has been as eloquent as any of these, in denouncing the inefficiency of English spelling. The book he completed before his death under the title 'The Case for Spelling Reform', bears two inscriptions: 'To the Schoolchildren of Britain—a Consistent Alphabet', and: 'To the Nations of the World—an International Language'. In his last years, Dr. Follick was inclined to think that the evaluation of alternative techniques of writing was primarily a task for linguistic studies (or, as he would say, for 'comparative philology'). In this, he was probably right. 'Primarily', however, must not be interpreted to mean 'exclusively'. It is important to realize that efficiency of communication is a social and psychological as well as a linguistic problem.

Linguistics provides the alphabet-maker with his principal tool—phonological analysis. But just as the engineer, who derives essential insights from physics, will yet not be able to decide on this basis alone what machines to build; so will the designer of alphabetic conventions find it impossible to decide, purely on linguistic grounds, what alphabet would be best in a given situation.

The problems of an English spelling-reform would have been solved long ago, if they were purely linguistic in character. It is not very difficult to devise a consistent alphabet (though it is not quite so easy as amateurs tend to think); and there is no shortage of such alphabets. But it is extremely difficult to devise one that has any chance of prevailing over the established tradition, and prevailing without causing more harm than good.

Techniques of writing and printing are a very special kind of technological equipment. To replace them is not nearly as easy as to replace some sort of machinery. In order to oust, say, the steam-engine, it was enough to have constructed a machine which could do the same job more efficiently. The scrapping of the old engines and of the plants producing them, and the re-training of a number of engineers and workers, must cause some harm and pain; but the harm will soon be healed, and the pain forgotten. The changes, on the other hand, which are called for by a new method of writing, are far more radical. A book lives much longer than any steam-engine; and every citizen has been trained a reader and writer, while only a few are experts in steam-engineering. The institution of English spelling is entrenched in countless private and public libraries, in thousands of schools and offices, in the special skills of many thousands of teachers, and of millions of people all over the world. Moreover, the particular Roman alphabet we use is clearly related to hundreds of similar alphabets, currently employed for the representation of other languages. In a technique of writing we are dealing with a ubiquitous kind of technological equipment: it is nothing less than the principal medium of a modern civilization, a constant link with our contemporaries as well as our ancestors.

The problem of spelling-reform cannot, therefore, be approached merely by asking whether we can devise a linguistically more adequate technique of writing. We certainly can. The question is also: Is it worth while?—As soon as we ask this question, the linguistically most adequate solutions—the 'best' alphabets—appear immediately to be impractical. We need not go so far as to exclude them for all time. Possibly, some day in the distant future, our economic and technical resources will permit a linguistically perfect spelling reform. Perhaps, some day, we shall be able and prepared to reprint the English texts in all libraries, private and public, all over the world. At present, however, a *perfect* convention for writing English needs only to be placed into the context of its prospective use, in order to be immediately rejected. This is why proposals for a spelling-reform cannot be judged by purely linguistic criteria. Having his 'perfect'

8

constructions rejected, the linguist will be asked to try again, and to come back with proposals within the limits of what is practicable.

Social conditions will then control the very construction of a revised script. The reformer will not be able to ward off such 'extraneous' considerations by any mere strategy of skilful campaigning. For the campaign itself, to be success-ful, asks for compromise. This becomes immediately clear, when we consider, how any proposed new script might come to be *adopted*, how it might issue in reform.

Most spelling-reformers agree that reform would have to be gradual. It would have to be carefully phased over a period of a few generations. What is true of every linguistic change—that the new must *co-exist* with the old before it prevails, would also be true of a reform of spelling-conventions. Even a reform by decree would have to simulate the gradual processes of natural linguistic change. There seems to be only one effective way of ensuring at least a temporary co-existence of new spelling-conventions with the old—namely, by teaching both in schools. This is why the campaign reported by Sir James Pitman—in the first lecture of this volume (pp.14ff.), and in greater detail, by Dr. Follick in his book—is of crucial interest. A Minister of Education had given permission for precisely such an experiment in co-existence; and it is being carried out with apparently increasing momentum to the present day.

There might have been some uncertainty, at first. Would a second alphabet be an additional burden for the children at school? Might it not confuse them? Indeed, such fears would have been well-founded, had the new script been linguistically perfect. But nothing of the sort has been attempted. The new alphabetic system which is now being taught in some primary schools is in fact a compromise with the old. And such a system has proved to be no burden at all. It has been shown—and this is, from the point of view of spelling-reform, the main contribution of Sir James Pitman's current experiments—that intrusion of a more consistent script of this sort will do no harm; there is even reason to believe that some such script could be of immediate use: it can make for an easier introduction to the traditional orthography, i.e. serve as an 'initial teaching alphabet'.

The first stage, then, in a reform of English spelling, could be almost painless. The initial co-existence of two alphabetic conventions can be cooperative rather than competitive, and yield immediate rewards in lightening the burden of learning to read and write, even with the given archaic tools. Indeed, nothing would be lost if the two conventions were to be kept side by side indefinitely—though, in that case, the ultimate greater gain of a reformed script would be forsaken.

Let us assume, then, that this would be the strategy of a spelling-reform—its progress to be channelled painlessly through its use as a transition-alphabet! It is clear that such a plan imposes severe restrictions on the reform itself. If the proposed new conventions are to be capable of serving as a first stage for acquiring the old, then any more extravagant novelty must be excluded. The Shaw alphabet (pp.120) would have no chance of being accepted as an 'initial teaching alphabet'.

How remarkable, then, that the only systematic script, so far, that has actually entered our schools as a transition alphabet—namely, Sir James Pitman's *i.t.a.*—does not claim to be a suitable candidate for spelling reform! Indeed, Sir James does not think that reform of English spelling should come by way of an initial teaching alphabet. In his opinion, a systematic script which is suitable for initial instruction in traditional orthography would 'thereby' be 'made less suitable for that other purpose'.—Now, it may well be true of *'i.t.a.'* that it would not be the best alphabet to serve both purposes. But the reason why Sir James considers the two functions to be incompatible is not to be found so much in the demands he makes on a transition-script as in the demands he makes on a spelling reform. This, he holds, should be on the lines of Bernard Shaw's proposals for a non-Roman alphabet, i.e. an alphabet totally different from our present techniques of writing.[1] Sir James's argument falls as soon as we abandon the idea of an uncompromising thorough-going reform. The auxiliary purpose of an initial teaching alphabet and the ultimate purpose of spelling reform are immediately compatible if we accept the general approach of Dr. Follick or Dr. Wijk or the Simplified Spelling Society who aim, all of them, at a reform 'with least disturbance' and, therefore, in the medium of the Roman script. Such a limited reform would permit precisely the kind of gradual transition and temporary co-existence which, through experiments with *i.t.a.*, has been proved to be educationally acceptable. For, it is *the same continuity with the tradition* that has to be preserved, on the one hand, if a revised alphabet is to serve as an easy introduction *to* the old, and, on the other, if it is to take over *from* the old without too much disturbance.

Of course, a viable compromise is more difficult to devise than a utopian new beginning. If proposals for a spelling reform were to be judged by phonological criteria alone, then some English script on the lines of the *International Phonetic Alphabet* (IPA) or even the *Shaw alphabet* would probably have been accepted long ago. If we stipulate that the new script should be produced by subjecting some standard form of English speech to a strictly phonemic analysis, then no controversial issue remains except the choice of suitable letter-shapes. This, as Mr. MacCarthy has shown,[2] is not a linguistic problem, but a complex of social, psychological, aesthetic and technological questions. Whatever the decision we should reach here, it would not interfere with the basic analysis itself, nor could it alter its findings. We should merely be asking how to *represent* the results of a given analysis.

The situation is radically different, if we regard a consistent phonetic script as altogether too deviant from the present orthography to serve the purposes of either primary school-teaching or reform, and prefer to seek a compromise of

1. I. J. Pitman, *Learning to Read* (Journal of the Royal Society of Arts, February 1961, p. 27).
2. See his paper on the Bernard Shaw Alphabet (pp. 105ff, below).

'least disturbance'. Then—and this does not seem to have been sufficiently realized—all kinds of social and psychological considerations must be brought in to influence the basic analysis itself, or to modify its results. The very criteria then by which we shall produce and judge a script, *are no longer capable of consistent application*: the whole task becomes a problem of *balancing conflicting claims*. Hence the difficulty of consistently applying 'guiding principles' such as those formulated by the Simplified Spelling Society. Mr. MacCarthy[1] has shown in fact how, in satisfying any of these principles, we are bound to contravene others. This issue must be faced squarely; or arguments for spelling reform will, as has happened so often, present themselves as just a welter of contradictions. Instead of pretending to some kind of deductive consistency, when we are in fact constantly and tacitly shifting our ground, we shall have to bring such shifts into the open, and acknowledge that our task is not to deduce a solution from first principles, but is the very different one of trying to attain a *state of balance*, precisely, on shifting ground.

It is from this point of view that Dr. Wijk's proposals[2] will be found to be especially interesting. At every step, the phonetician or linguist is called upon to decide how much he may reasonably concede to sociological, psychological, and pedagogical considerations. *Some* concessions are bound to be made. This is no longer the comparatively easy task of deducing solutions from general principles, but the highly controversial task of judging every single revision on its merits, and adjudicating upon conflicting claims. Nevertheless, we are not reduced to unreasoned intuitive decisions. On the contrary: rival claims must be clearly stated and the limits of compromise be accurately defined.

1. *See* below, *New Spelling With Old Letters*, pp. 89–104.
2. *See* below, *Regularized English*, pp. 50–88. Of the systems presented in this volume, Dr. Wijk's seems to be less widely known than the others. In a recent publication (*Studies in Spelling*, University of London Press, 1961), Dr. W. Boyd called for precisely the kind of minimal reform which has been worked out by Dr. Wijk in his 'Regularized English'.

Problems of 'spelling reform' demand a great deal of further study; and some later volumes in this series will be devoted to an investigation of them. The present volume may serve as a useful introduction: the problems to be dealt with emerge naturally from reviewing some of the more important English alphabets so far proposed. The following papers are, in effect, such a review.

Sir James Pitman's paper presents the system of English spelling which he designed as an Initial Teaching Alphabet —'*i.t.a.*'. A comparison with Dr. Follick's alphabet leads him to examine how different social and educational aims will determine the design of different scripts.

Mr. Peter MacCarthy (of the Department of Phonetics in the University of Leeds) discusses some important technical alternatives, among which any spelling reform of English would have to choose; and he explains the principles which were adopted in the design of the two very different reform proposals—the Simplified Spelling Society's 'New Spelling', and the 'Bernard Shaw Alphabet'.

Dr. Axel Wijk (of the University of Stockholm) presents a system of 'Regularized English', which may be described as a proposal for minimal reform and maximal continuity.

# 2

# The late Dr. Mont Follick— an appraisal

## The Assault on the Conventional Alphabets and Spelling

*by*

Sir James Pitman K.B.E.

IT is a great honour to give the Inaugural Mont Follick Lecture, as well as an opportunity. It is indeed a great honour to be invited to the University of Manchester: it is moreover a great opportunity to be able thus to promote, to this learned and important audience, the concepts which he clearly saw, strongly advocated during his life,[1] and richly endowed at his death.

Dr. Follick (Labour, Loughborough) and I were not only colleagues in the House of Commons from 1945 until his withdrawal from politics in 1955 but we worked there together (he Labour and I Conservative) on this dearly-held objective of his. Late in November 1958 I had visited him in hospital. This was very shortly before his death, which took place on 10th December. He was feeling well, and was in fine spirits. But this was, alas, a misplaced optimism. I had called for social reasons,[2] and about his intended book,[3] but he started to discuss his Will and his hopes that, by founding a Chair at a University, his intentions might be better carried out, notwithstanding his death, and possibly even better

The numbers refer to the Notes towards the end and the letters to the sources, given in the Bibliography.

14

because of his death. It is curious to recall that yet another life-long believer in the need for a new and better medium for reading and writing—no less than the great George Bernard Shaw—placed a similar reliance upon testamentary action. It is thus even more curious still that I should have found myself involved—in Shaw's case by specific request in writing,[4] and in Follick's virtually on his death-bed—in acting as 'watch-dog' for the Wills of both of them.

In the event, there must have been something about men so convinced of the strength of this power of willing. In their lives they had been most effective in this almost impossibly difficult field, and in their deaths they have thus continued, and become even more so. Certainly Mont Follick has been equal to Shaw in effectiveness and success—at any rate in the first two of the four successive stages through which the objective, which he shared with Shaw (and with myself), must pass if it is to achieve the aim intended.

The first of these stages is to establish generally, and in the minds of responsible, and indeed influential, citizens, that the letters and characters we now employ are only conventional, and only imperfectly so, having been evolved no less than two thousand years ago by a foreign people who spoke only their own foreign language, and that those characters are consequently likely to be unsuitable for, and thus a handicap to, written communication in our English language: that they are indeed insufficient and inefficient for their intended purpose.

The second stage is to inform them that there are indeed an infinity of ways in which English might be otherwise conventionally printed and written, and further that a chosen new medium need not supersede, and thus displace, the old but may enjoy a parallel currency; that just as the uncial letter, stroked on parchment by quill pens, e.g. a, and the cursive letter pushed in all directions on paper by the new steel-pointed nibs, e.g. ɑ, have not superseded but have paralleled the upper-case letter, A, originally carved in stone pediments by Roman chisels and mallets, so a new convention based upon a better appreciation of the needs of written

15

communication in English may yet become conventional and, when so used, need not displace the three existing alphabets (which differ so greatly from one another—e.g. A a a B b $\ell$) but offer a further and wholly suitable and thus efficient convention for optional parallel use.

The third stage is to persuade some authoritative body to investigate the question, and to demonstrate, beyond further discussion, what precisely will be the advantages in accepting a particular alternative convention for parallel use.

The fourth is to gain for such new convention a wide, and ever widening, acceptance by readers, and use by writers and printers, so that the new visual convention may enjoy as complete a general acceptance as is enjoyed by the spoken convention, and a use at least as wide, *even if selective for occasion*, as those uses now enjoyed by our three presently accepted conventions:

Aaɑ: Bb$\ell$: C: Dd: Ee: F$\mathscr{F}$f$f$ :

etc.—which are used variously for *selective* occasions.

These were his objectives—and he was a single-minded propagandist for them. As early as 1914 he had written a book about it, published later in 1934[c]. On 22nd August 1945, within only nine Parliamentary days of his entry to the House, he had extended the venue to Parliament with a maiden speech[d] on this subject, and on his death-bed he laid it as his charge upon the administrators of his will.

Ever lucky in Parliamentary ballots, he became entitled to initiate on 6th March 1952 a debate on the Navy Estimates and chose, to the amusement of all, the benefits of Simplified English Spelling to the Royal Navy in its communications.

His objective appeared quite irrelevant to the Navy Estimates yet we managed, he and I, without breaking the rules of order, to debate the Royal Navy's communication system in relation to the speech of the eleven nationalities seeking to operate efficiently together in N.A.T.O., in terms of the need for an alphabeticism and a code system which might better allow non-English-speaking sailors to make themselves understood, when converting into speech over the

16

radio-telephone or the loud-hailer, what had been handed to them as written messages in English.[5]

In season—sometimes thus on the border of being out of season—he pursued his first aim, the aim of bringing to the attention of all that a change in our conventions for writing and printing could greatly benefit the world and us.

His good fortune in the ballot in Parliament for Private Members' Bills also was phenomenal. Out of over 600 members he twice drew lucky in the annual ballot, and thus gained the opportunity to introduce a Bill, and on both occasions with the certainty that there would be sufficient Parliamentary time to enable it to be debated at length and, *if accepted*, to reach the Statute Book. His first, debated on 11th March 1949,[g] was defeated on second reading by only 3 votes (84 Ayes to 87 Noes) after a five-hour debate; and the second,[m] on 27th February 1953, was successful, to the astonishment of all, by 12 votes (65 Ayes to 53 Noes) after an equally full debate. It was, moreover, further successful in Committee Stage, against the bitter opposition not only of the then Conservative Minister of Education but also of Mr. Chuter Ede, the leader of the Labour contingent.[6] Incredible as it may seem, this success had been achieved notwithstanding that the Whips of both sides were active against the Bill. Nevertheless, the Bill survived and was agreed to be reported to the House, after a most exciting tie on the voting over a "wrecking" amendment in Committee, when the Chairman, in a moment of high drama, cast his vote in favour of the Bill.[n & r]

Much "horse trading" then took place behind the scenes before the next stage—the Report Stage. The Minister—and, it was said, the Cabinet no less so—remained bitterly antagonistic to us. On the other hand, a third defeat of the Minister on Report Stage (which was the humiliation which was confidently foretold in the gossip of the Smoking Room) would have been a most damaging set-back for the Minister personally, and an acute embarrassment for the Government, even though the House of Commons at the Third Reading, or at worst the House of Lords, could have been depended upon to kill the Bill eventually. On our side was this certainty that defeat would indeed eventually catch up on the miraculously surviving product of back-bench independence and intransigence, and the hope that the Minister might be persuaded, in saving face, to concede what was the substance of the Bill, by an official reply to a Parliamentary Question to be tabled by Dr. Follick. The horse trading continued. The Minister was obdurate and Follick impracticably sanguine, and both were against any such deal. I had played a very active part in this Bill—indeed, Follick had given me the opportunity to draft it and to conduct it through the House as if I, not he, had been the winner in the ballot. I had thus been negotiating with the Minister and consulting with Dr. Follick and with a number particularly of his Labour supporters. They joined me in advising Follick to accept the substance, if not the form, of total victory, and not to court an inevitable anti-climax of final defeat from which nothing could be gained and little rescued, not even the honour and glory, nor even the other and more practical benefits which were being offered. Eventually the terms were agreed and Follick handed in at the Table a withdrawal of his Bill, and an agreed Question (directed to that point alone which was the essence of the Bill) to which the Minister had already promised the answer:—

MR. FOLLICK asked the Minister of Education her policy towards proposals by a competent research organization to investigate possible improvements in the teaching of reading by means of a system of simplified spelling.

MISS HORSBRUGH: Any such organization could rely on my interest and good will for their proposal, as for any proposal designed to investigate possible improvements in this field of education. Such interest and good will would not imply any prospect of additional grant. It would be for the organization concerned to secure the willing co-operation of local education authorities, teachers and parents, as these must in my view remain free to decide with what particular forms of research they wish to associate themselves. All concerned in any such researches could rest assured of my good wishes for their work.

(Hansard 7th May 1953)[p]

This 'good will' and 'interest' meant everything; and they were in the event to prove their worth. Moreover, the value

18

and importance of gaining this opportunity for investigating Follick's and my theory, under Local Education Authority auspices and with Ministerial backing, cannot be exaggerated. It was thus of the greatest possible worth for the most important third stage of obtaining an authoritative trial—worth even more and of even more importance than the stir which had been created in respect of the first two stages. On the Minister's side the reservation about 'money' meant nothing: nor did that about 'willing co-operation of Local Education Authorities, teachers and parents.' These were "face savers" because from the beginning, assurances had been given that the provision for a diversion of moneys from the public funds, then being paid to the money-starved National Foundation for Educational Research in England and Wales (the Foundation then received from Government funds only £5,000 for all research into education in the whole of England and Wales), had been no more than an inevitable expediency, a meaningless procedural device for bringing the Bill within the very restricted rules of Order applicable to Private Members' Bills. In any case money from the Government rather than from the Research Foundation's already ear-marked funds would have been well deserved and most remuneratively invested, as was shown by later results, but Dr. Follick and I were realists enough not to have pressed for it when once the Government hostility had become so great and obvious. The requirement about the voluntary collaboration on the part of all parties had already been written into the Bill.[7]

What clearly was of the greatest importance was that defeat had not been suffered and that this official promise of 'interest and good will' and the expression of 'good wishes,' and co-operation in any research, which had been extracted against bitter opposition, had been a considerable victory.

The outcome was thus an unexpected triumph for Dr. Follick where all, not only the many scornful, had predicted inevitable failure. It had been too, a magnificent parade before the public of the fact that his concept was not merely lively but potentially viable; but best of all it had made

19

possible and virtually begun the advance along the essential road of demonstrating convincingly to those who mattered, the rightness of the case and the great potential value of his aim, Shaw's and mine, not only to the English-speaking world but also to the would-be English-speaking world.

It was very sad that, later, a mirage of still greater triumph should have appeared to Dr. Follick, and should thus have turned sour his hour of triumph—and so soon after the great success he had achieved. Although he had supported me in a joint statement of jubilant satisfaction (*See* note *r* and page 37) and some days later had written in similarly satisfied terms to *The Times* (*See* note *q* and page 38), he later came to regret what he had done in withdrawing his Bill while still alive; and, in brooding on it, he came to resent the agreement with me and his other friends by which we had negotiated for him and agreed with the Minister, and to deplore his withdrawal, and to suppose, bitterly, that he had been over-persuaded in a situation in which the Bill could have been carried, not only through its remaining Report and Third Reading in the Commons, but even through all stages in the House of Lords. This was an impossibility, but the sad fact is that he came to believe it possible—indeed certain. He thus never savoured for long, or sufficiently, the sweets of his great if not absolute success, nor appreciated how far he and I had gone to achieve progress in as many as three of the four successive stages necessary for ultimate success. Firstly he had advertised through the English-speaking world, and indeed throughout non-English-speaking countries too, that the English language as presently printed with the old roman alphabet was no longer thought to be perfect and above improvement, even in its own home land. Secondly he had forced the Government, and the particular Minister most influential in English literate activities, to agree that the traditional conventions might be challenged to trial to justify their dominance in Infant teaching at any rate, and to promise to give moral support to the act of challenge whenever it might be mounted. Thirdly he had in this paved the way for the eventual action by a major British University[8]—the leading Institute of Education and the only body important enough to dare stage such a challenge and, having staged it, to dare to adjudicate the winner. He had thus carried the cause from the negative phase of decrying the old as being bad, to the positive one of introducing and testing a to-be-newly-created and better alternative.

Meanwhile, Bernard Shaw, who was alive during the first of Dr. Follick's Bills, had supported him, if with certain reservations.[9] Moreover, Shaw's support after his (Shaw's) death was most effective, not only in his Will and in the bitter contesting of it, but also in the *de facto* victory on Appeal against the earlier adverse decision in the Lower Court. (See Weekly Law Report.[8]) Shaw had thus been very active in supporting Follick's and my objective, particularly for that first stage of their objective, a stage in which all were wholly at one. Just as the earlier news that the British Parliament had voted in favour of a new spelling had made front-page headlines in the British and overseas Press, so too, each of these three successive propaganda explosions of the dead, but still living, G.B.S. achieved, if possible, even bigger, better and wider world Press coverage, and discussion.

No one could any longer maintain that consideration of a new convention and a better medium was other than a lively one. It might be stupid, it might be a lot else besides, but it was very lively. Generally in the minds of all, responsible or not, influential or not, was an awareness that a new force had arisen, one no longer to be ridiculed and airily dismissed; they became aware of the advent of a new medium of communication, which might be seen, if no bigger than a man's hand rising as a cloud on the horizon, bringing with it the possibility of the new and the better. The uninfluential did not know how, or why, a new and better was thus on the horizon; the influential, virtually all, pre-judged the result of the challenge and were certain that the new would not be better—and reconciled themselves to the tiresome period of disturbance apparently necessary for proving them right. Meanwhile, let sleep be disturbed as little as possible, for after all what hope was there of finding any University, much

21

less a major one, so bereft of its senses and so blind to the decencies of cultured communication, as to be willing, much less desirous, of setting up the lists for such a challenge and acting as the organizer of the challenge and as the judge?

We should thus recognize the enormous importance of this great achievement in Dr. Follick's struggle—for it had been a struggle indeed. Aided as he may have been by Shaw and by me, without him there could hardly in our generation have been the foundation of the first two stages and the opportunity for others to pass to the third—and for yet others even later to reach within aiming distance of the fourth and final stage.

It is in the passing from the second, and general, stage, to the third and particular stage, that variety and therefore differences and troubles begin. The unity in emphasizing the faults of our accidental, undesigned, unsuitable and thus inefficient medium is considerable, but it is at the point of proceeding to the next stage, the particularized stage, that the field of disagreement seems to open as wide as the field of alternatives which then compete for the opportunity of trial, for the chance to show success in demonstration, for hopes both of a proven superiority and thus of a general acceptance, and of the final accolade of world-wide use.

In the choice of which of many possible new conventions should be tried, Dr. Follick placed the *learning* process, and the learning process *for the foreigner* who does not speak English, as the factor for improvement.[10] Shaw, however, placed the day-to-day *using* process, and the using process by *those who were already skilled* in the reading, writing, listening to and speaking of English, as the only significant factor for the desired improvement.[11] Follick saw some value for benefit in use when learned, but since he was working primarily for those other than the already-English-speaking people he insisted that what must be learnt must sufficiently resemble English as normally printed for it to be immediately read by those literate in their own romanic languages and spellings, and that it was the spelling only with the roman alphabet which needed alteration for improvement, not the roman alphabet itself. He thus made the issue one of reform of

22

existing spelling, using the existing alphabet, where Shaw regarded the need as being one of reform of the roman alphabet, a reform indeed so radical as to depart from it.

In consequence, just as Shaw insisted that only a departure from the inherited disadvantages of the past could give a significant improvement in daily performance,[12 & 15] so Follick and I insisted that only a retention of it could best help in the *learning* period—if it could be assumed that the old medium would inevitably continue and would thus for ever need to be learned. My own view was, and is, to sympathize and agree with both attitudes, regarding them both as good, *and moreover as non-conflicting.* Certainly if it is a case of helping the learning of the existing conventions, the factor of a high degree of compatibility between any new convention and the old is vitally important. Moreover, I regard the teaching of the English child, and acceptability by the English, as in any case a paramount need.

Shaw did not deny benefit in the learning process, but insisted that benefit in use when learned would be considerable, but would be obtained only if the unhappy legacy from Rome were to be thrown overboard and the designer of the new *and additional* convention be allowed a clean sheet. He argued that the benefit would need to be indeed considerable, if any generalized use and acceptance were to be hoped for, and that only by bursting wide open all restrictions on design, and allowing a complete departure from the original roman upper-case alphabet and its later evolutions, could a modern designer achieve a fresh representation of English which would be sufficiently more beneficial in use to win general adoption,[13] and, in doing so, to close the gap in speed, convenience and cost which now separates a spoken communication from a written one, and even more from a printed one.[14]

Dr. Follick concentrated on the value of the alphabet in learning. This is certainly *a* most constructive policy because it is during the learning period, not during the period of use, that lies the advantage of man's undeniably great invention of the alphabet. Indeed few recognize that the invention of the alphabet has done nothing to help reading once reading has become skilled, and little, if anything, to help writing, once the learner has become skilful and habituated as a writer. The alphabet *per se* is thus crucial for learning, the design of particular characters crucial for expedition in use.

Shaw thus on his side, rightly, insisted that *only* a departure from the familiar—a departure, moreover, no less great than that from longhand to shorthand or than that from roman numerals to arabic ones[15]—could offer a sufficiently great benefit in day-to-day use to deserve and win a popular preference from the writer as a 'manual laborer' in his everyday use, and that such a departure from the old roman convention would impose in practice a strain on learning much less than is generally, and wrongly, supposed, and only an insignificant task in transferring to and from other alphabetic patterns.[16] There have been, however, few who have as yet followed him in this grand approach, involving as might appear an abandonment of the roman alphabet and an inability to read the new medium with immediate transfer—even though the transfer may with no serious labour be effortlessly achieved later.[17]

Dr. Follick and I were determined that, be that as it may, however right Shaw might be in his approach, nevertheless the simplification of the roman alphabet designed to help those learning our present romanic systems of communication was at least of equal, and indeed of over-riding, importance, and ought to be the first approach. However right Shaw may have been, and be yet proved to have been, there would *always* remain a use for the roman alphabet and a need thus to learn it more successfully and with less effort: and the need to help those who wished to learn English in its spoken and in its conventionally printed forms. Certainly, therefore, the two concepts were not in the long run in conflict, and in our view at any rate and that of the vast majority, it was more timely to seek first to improve the use of the existing alphabet and thus to help all in the *learning* stages, whether of reading or of English as a second language, than to attempt as yet the crossing of the gulf to a new and non-romanic alphabet.

Dr. Follick was founder and proprietor of the Regent

24

School of Languages, London,[e] and thus his first interest was to help the foreigner seeking to speak and read English: mine has always been to help the already-English-speaking child in learning to read and write. Dr. Follick claimed that a systematic alphabeticism designed to help the foreigner would also help the English-speaking child: I could claim that, whereas that was no doubt true, the reverse would be no less true. The choice of priority between these two judgments thus lay at the centre of a decision on which of two policies for the design of the new medium should be adopted for testing, because any advance to the third stage would necessitate *a* decision on medium, and this in turn would require a determination of purpose and a corresponding specification. Which, then, of these differing priorities should be preferred? Which should be the purpose?[18]

All will be agreed with Dr. Follick's conviction that the English language was capable of great expansion in world use, and that a close relationship of English print through the alphabet, to the print of other languages, would be helpful to that end. Moreover such a close relationship would help those speakers of other languages rather than mislead them when they learnt our language from books and would thus greatly increase the speed of that expansion. How, may it be asked, will those who read from books suppose that the dis-related words such as *once*, *ought*, *all*, *was* (cp. *has*), should be pronounced? English-speaking children begin at their mother's knee to learn language first as a spoken tongue. They thus learn to speak first and only later to read, whereas those who come to English as a second language mostly learn from books, and thus need either to reverse the order or to learn both together (possibly most beneficially) in a close time relationship between the one and the other. For those who learn English as a second language it is in either case the eye more than the ear which carries the lesson, a lesson which will be misleading to the ear, unless there be the desired closer relationship between print and speech.

Dr. Follick further regarded the alphabetic practices of those who already read and write Spanish, German, French, and other European languages, and their particular variants of roman alphabeticism (particularly Spanish), as those alphabetic practices which ought to be preferred. He thus considered that it should be their practice which should determine the purpose and specification for the design of any new medium.

By contrast others, such as Robert Bridges, Sir Gilbert Murray, Arthur Lloyd James, Daniel Jones and I, have regarded as our primary concern those whose first language is English, and have regarded the present spelling of English, rather than those of French, Spanish, German, etc., as the starting point for any new medium to be designed to help the learner, whether English-speaking or not.

Fortunately for our good relations, Dr. Follick, while he was didactic over the policy for a specification which would serve the foreigner first, was not anxious to press the issue to any point even approaching conflict. His idea of a University acting as his instrument for decision provided that they, not he, would settle the detail of the alphabet when he was dead, and covered his expectation that they would certainly agree with his preference.[19]

The difference in the intended beneficiary and thus in the approach, and consequently the medium, is set out below:[20]

*The Beneficiary:*

*Follick's:*

The foreigner, particularly those literate in the roman alphabet (and in Spanish even more particularly).

*Pitman's i.t.a.:*

The young illiterate English-speaking child.

*The Intention and Approach:*

*Follick's:*

To teach English, listening and speech and reading and writing.

*Pitman's i.t.a.:*

To teach reading and writing and develop language.

*The Medium :*

*Follick's and Pitman's i.t.a. :*

The following 23 single characters (and sounds thereby represented) are common to both. Moreover there is common agreement that all these 23 should retain their most usual sound value in English orthography:

a,[21] b, c,[22] d, e, f, g, h, i, j, (k), l, m, n, o, p, r, s, t, u, v, w,[22] z.

The following table completes the two alphabets of 37 and 40* sounds respectively—

| | Follick | | | Pitman's i.t.a. | |
|---|---|---|---|---|---|
| ei | pein | (pain) | 24 | æ | pæn |
| ie | hie | (he) | 25 | єє | hєє |
| ai | waild | (wild) | 26 | ie | wield |
| ou | ouver | (over) | 27 | œ | œver |
| iu | dispiut | (dispute) | 28 | ue | dispuet |
| oa | poazt | (paused) | 29 | au | pausd |
| au | hau | (how) | 30 | ou | hou |
| oi | emploiment | | 31 | oi | emploiment |
| uu | intuu | (into) | 32 | ω | intω |
| | ruumert | (rumoured) | 33 | ω | rωmerd |
| aa | Maarz | (Mars) | 34 | a | mars |
| sh | shie | (she) | 35 | ʃh | ʃhєє |
| th | thin | | 36 | ţh | ţhin |
| dh | dhu | (the) | 37 | ţh | ţhe |
| zh | azhiur | (azure) | 38 | ʒ | aʒuer |
| ng | fieling | (feeling) | 39 | ŋ | feeliŋ |
| tsh | mutsh | (much) | 40 | ʤ | muʤ |
| | iet | (yet) | 41 | y | yet |
| | huen | (when) | 42 | wh | when |
| | haz | (has) | 43 | s | has |
| | | | 44 | ɾ | her[24] |
| | | | | a | ask[23] |

* Note. The total of 40 sounds is reconciled by adding the sound at No. 41 and deducting that of *c* (or *k*) from the 23 "retentions".

3

27

Here, then, is the specimen passage as printed in Follick's 'The Influence of English,' page 131; and below, the same passage printed in *i.t.a.*—with below again the same passage printed in the Shaw Alphabet:—

'Ei tuisted flash ov pein shot akros dhu peinter's feis. Hie poazt for ei moment, and ei waild fieling ov piti keim ouver him ¿ After oal, huot rait had hie tuu prai intuu dhu laif ov Dorian Grei? ¡ If hie had dun ei taidh ov huot uos ruumert abaut him, hau mutsh hie must have sufert! Dhen hie streitent himself up and uokt ouver tuu dhu fairpleis, and stuud dher, luuking at dhu burning logs uith dheir frost-laik ashes and dheir throbing corz ov fleim.'[25]

'a twisted flaſh ov pæn ſhot across ꝥe pænter's fæs. hɛɛ pausꝺ for a mœment and a wielꝺ fɛɛliŋ ov pity cæm œver him. after aul, whot riet haꝺ hɛɛ tœ prie intœ ꝥe lief ov ꝺorian græ? if hɛɛ haꝺ ꝺun a tieſh ov whot woſ rœmerꝺ about him, hou muꝇh hɛɛ must hav sufferꝺ! ꝥen hɛɛ strætend himself up anꝺ waukt œver tœ ꝥe fierplæs anꝺ stœꝺ ꝥær, lœkiŋ at ꝥe burniŋ logſ wiꝥ ꝥær frost-liek aſheſ anꝺ ꝥær ꝥrobbiŋ corſ ov flæm.'

[Shaw alphabet text]

The specimen in the Shaw alphabet is identical in size of type and in spacing to those of the other two. The difference in length illustrates the saving in space (but not necessarily—and certainly not necessarily proportionately—in speed of reading and of writing) which may be achieved by such a departure from the romanic legacy.

The difference in these three specimens high-lights the difference of approach. Follick's first priority, as the intended beneficiary, is the already literate foreigner: mine, the as yet illiterate English-speaking child: Shaw's the 'Author as

28

Manual Laborer' (*sic*) and other practising literates—about which proposed approach more later.

Follick and I were always very friendly in discussing that difference and thus in supporting the main policy which we each favoured, if not the detail for its implementation. In this we nevertheless both respected the point of view of the other, in our conflicting priorities. This could well be so, seeing that in both Bills the determination of the new medium was to be left to others—and at a later date. I considered that we must begin aiming at home before we could possibly hope to go overseas—whereas he took the opposite view.

It now appears, as may be supposed from the successful trial and increasing use of *i.t.a.*, that we are unlikely ever to find out whether Dr. Follick's views ought to have prevailed or not. In the event, my case for starting at home has seemed to many to be the stronger of the two—at any rate, if it be desired that we make a start at all.[26] Better to have achieved a start with a new medium, less perfect for the one use if more perfect for the other, than never to have achieved a start at all. This practical consideration seemed to me to be crucial to any action—and thus to the opportunity of reaching the third and fourth stages—the third of investigating, of demonstrating, and of adjudicating, and the fourth and final stage of being accorded the accolade of conventional acceptance and use for the purpose intended—in my case, a very limited purpose.

I was convinced that only in the country of origin of the English language could the opportunity be won to pass onward to the two last stages and to turn theory into practice, and so win general acceptance, and that even a leading foreign university would be unable to win acceptance in English-speaking countries, or in general, for a better medium, however demonstrably better that medium might have been proved overseas to have been. That which is read and written in Britain, Ireland, America, Canada, Australia, New Zealand and South Africa is the inevitable norm, and no departure or even supplement to our present orthography could be contemplated which had not been approved and adopted by those

29

who set the norm, that is to say, those who read and write it as their native literacy.

Moreover, it was most unlikely that any new medium could gain acceptance, even outside the English-speaking communities, unless it were then known to be a version of English acceptable in England. What would be rejected by the English as not English could never be worth learning, and would be rejected also by those seeking to learn English, who would thus come to regard their efforts in learning through that new medium, as a mis-direction and a waste of their time and of much laborious effort.

Moreover, there would arise, particularly in the developing countries, the question—Is this real English or is it a special sub-standard version designed for my supposedly lesser abilities? A sub-standard version, moreover, which will be a continuing shame, as evidence of my inability to stand as an equal with the rest of the English-speaking peoples?

It seemed to me that only if a new English medium were to start in England, and were anyhow to be seen, even in England, to be no more than a transitional learning medium, and to become accepted there as one clearly designed only as a means of *learning* the traditional orthography of English, could there be any hope of persuading a German or a Ghanaian willingly to accept it as the object of his many hours of study.

I must not be misunderstood into implying that Dr. Follick regarded his medium as one leading to the traditional medium. He was indeed an out-and-out spelling reformer—one who wished to see the old utterly superseded and indeed abolished, and never seen again except as a curiosity of earlier times in libraries and museums. He wanted the new to replace the old completely. He envisaged all books to be reprinted—indeed, he never envisaged any other course. It has been only Bernard Shaw, the American Dr. Edwin Leigh and I who have drawn a distinction which would allow the old to continue, as roman numerals have, while yet introducing the new in a supplementing parallelism. We three alone have thus seen the new as a supplementing parallel rather than as a destroying substitution.[27a] Shaw was aware that no one

30

already *skilled* in reading and writing in the roman alphabet and in our traditional orthography, would tolerate both a major disturbance of his visual habituations and a virtual destruction of all his hardly acquired skills in automatized writing—a disturbance of the conditioned practice of reception and of emission and thus an assault upon the emotions. He recognized that any attempt to persuade the literate man-in-the-street even to accept—much less to become enthusiastically active about—such a major disturbance and destruction of his skills was as utterly hopeless as the operation itself would be—in his opinion anyhow—utterly useless at the end. What was needed was not a destruction, or even disturbance, of the old by the new, but the development of a new reading and writing medium, the new to be continued as heretofore side by side with a continuance of the old. The new would need to be, and could with little difficulty be, significantly better for the communicator when writing, and possibly also for the to-be-communicated-with in reading (as distinct from being better only as a learning medium), than the old.[27b] Shaw insisted that parallel alphabeticisms could and would very happily co-exist and that, if the new were to be brought into existence, and if it were to afford major benefits in use, it would come to be more and more used, just as arabic numerals have come to be accepted because they are more beneficial in use, and in the end are preferred to the roman numerals which continue nevertheless. Benefit in use for the new in contrast with the wastefulness and inefficiency of the old, to be demonstrated in pounds, shillings and pence (and converted also into dollars) should be the note to be struck: the stimulus of cash value in the more efficient medium should be the key to success.[28]

Dr. Follick was an opinionated man on his own special subject. So too was Shaw; and I would not dissent from the application of that epithet to me, at any rate in respect of that same subject! Fortunately, Follick and I were able to agree to differ about the final and as yet hypothetical stages, each of us convinced that we could enthusiastically collaborate in the activities of the first stage; that is to say, we were in full agreement that all activities directed to undermining the supposed efficiency and sacrosanctity of the present orthography were grist to the mill of both of us. We both of us meanwhile reserved our prophetic fears of future difference, in the supposition that the definitive choice would be taken not during our joint lifetimes, and thus by others! Moreover, we were each free to suppose that those who would be making the choice, if that day were ever to come, would have the intelligence and judgment to make the right choice, disagreeing with the one and agreeing with the other—or finding and choosing yet a third!

His solicitor and I made a very small congregation at Golders Green Crematorium on 16th December 1958. Seldom has a man been laid to rest so apparently with absolutely nothing of his life-compelling intentions accomplished. However, that was only how it then appeared. So often is the short view a wrong one.

Whenever historians come to assess those steps in the upward progress of mankind which have been the most important, the palm must always go to that brilliant first step —to language itself. They will then recognize three almost comparable steps and human achievements, to be thus subsequently greatly honoured.

First came the invention of writing and the alphabet and the anonymous man—or rather men—who started the first and improved it with the second. There were no doubt two successive groups of men. The first group recognized that speech was evanescent and that a permanent record was desirable. The second recognized that a host of arbitrary ideograms to represent different concepts without reference to the sound of such words when spoken in association with the concepts was an unnecessary burden. Such spoken words are after all necessarily the linguistic starting point of anyone seeking to communicate efficiently in writing with anyone else in his own language group. It was they who, recognizing the need, invented the alphabet and thus achieved a sufficiently systematic relationship between the existing spoken conventions and the written conventions which were to be created.

This was the second great advance. Those men must also have recognized that *scripta manent*, while *verba volant*. They would have appreciated that alphabetic writing would eventually not only make communication permanent instead of fugitive and evanescent but also would substantially help and extend the other and spoken medium, and thus facilitate, extend and indeed perfect, communication by word of mouth as well as by word of pen—just as, at the beginning, speech had created the written form.

On the foundation of this means of recording knowledge and thus giving permanency to man's discoveries, and of affording subsequent access to it, was built the edifice of the accumulation of man's knowledge, and the opportunity for man, in succeeding generations, to climb up on the shoulders of all his predecessors, and in adding to that knowledge to pass an ever-growing accumulation to his successors.

Next came the invention of printing, and in this case we are too inclined to heap the whole credit upon the man Gutenberg. He was, however, no more than one in the line of those who introduced the factor of *multiplication* and enabled a number of *identical* copies of sheets, bearing printed words, to be made.[29] On this factor of multiplication has been based the *spread* of man's accumulated knowledge, regardless of distance, time and population. The alphabet has thus been given the soil in which the tree of knowledge, in growing and expanding, might bear fruit and multiply.

The third to be honoured will be a band of men, among whom Follick will rank high: those who, rejected and spurned by the majority since the days of Sir Thomas Smith,[30] conceived, worked and persisted in the face of all difficulties to introduce into the English language, as hitherto written and printed, that factor of a *closely* systematic alphabetic relationship, which, though present in the potential of alphabeticism, has hitherto been denied both to those who speak the English language and to those who do not, but wish to do so. It may confidently be predicted that on this factor of a closer, indeed a very close, relationship, will be built a world currency for the English language and a host of other

33

outstanding social consequences of world importance, all based upon the more efficient communication which the application of a helpful rather than a misleading alphabeticism will bring about. Follick's achievement in winning Government approval for the trial of a truly alphabetic representation of English is thus rightly to be recorded and honoured, at this his inaugural lecture.

## NOTES

1. In a similar situation in 1945, Dr. Follick used the following words: 'I have come here this evening to try to stir up in this conference an idea of the importance of this change in our alphabet.'[e]
Dr. Follick would have wished, indeed insisted, that I use this occasion of the Inaugural Lecture and of a highly intelligent, responsible and influential audience to draw attention to the need for, and great importance of, change in our alphabeticism.

2. Dr. Follick had written (in a letter of 10th November 1958) inviting me to 'have lunch together for the sake of old times.'

3. Under the title of *The Case for Spelling Reform*, which is now published by Sir Isaac Pitman & Sons, with a foreword by Sir William Mansfield Cooper, Vice Chancellor of the University of Manchester.

4. Extracts from letter from George Bernard Shaw to Mr. I. J. Pitman dated 19th July 1944 (see particularly the last paragraph)—

'This is to report progress, and may be read at your convenience.

'My circular letter to government departments, colleges, societies, trusts, and all the other stones I could think of to turn, has, with one exception, elicited nothing but letters, mostly polite and even sympathetic, but all to the same effect: "An interesting project, but not our job."

'The one exception is The Association of Scientific Workers at 73 High Holborn. They write "The Executive Committee are wholeheartedly in support of your proposal for research into the design of a more adequate British alphabet, and for propagating its desirability...."

'I am therefore directing that my residuary estate shall accumulate for 20 years (the perpetuity limit) and be available meanwhile for financing certain exactly defined and limited operations: to wit (a) designing a new British one-sound-one-letter alphabet, (b) the transliteration into it of two or three masterpieces of English literature, including two of my own plays, and (c) the publication of these transliterations and depositing of copies in leading public libraries throughout the Commonwealth and elsewhere. And that is all.

34

"Financing" includes payment of designers, adapters of composing and printing machines, phonetic experts for the transliteration etc. etc. etc. The availability of the money and its object to be advertized periodically by the Public Trustee. If nothing happens, or the bequest fails through any cause, I have provided alternative destinations for the money which will prevent its being left "in the air" in any case. And I shall have given the alphabet question a good standing advertisement for 20 years.

'And so I wash my hands of the business, and leave the field open to you to do the job with a grant-in-aid from the Public Trustee under the Shaw bequest if you care to. You are, I should say, by far the best equipped adventurer in the field.'

5. The terms of the Motion were—

This House is of opinion that a great advantage would accrue, in the sending of dispatches, signals, orders and messages, if some simplification of the English spelling were introduced.

(Hansard: Thursday 6th March 1952)[j]

6. There is a commentary on the proceedings of the 1953 Bill by William Barkley (the well-known Parliamentary Correspondent for the Daily Express and the author of *The Two Englishes* 1941; *Bad Language* 1946; *A Last Word* 1961) in the Summer 1953 issue of *The Pioneer*,[r] the Bulletin of the Simplified Spelling Society, of which the following extract is relevant—

'In the absence of Miss Florence Horsbrugh, The Minister, Mr. Kenneth Pickthorn, the Under-secretary, put the official line—despite frequent correction—that the Bill was an attempt to impose a curriculum and teaching methods centrally upon schools.

'Other teachers supported the Bill but its strongest opponent was one of Mr. Pickthorn's predecessors in office, Mr. Chuter Ede, who sought to ridicule the whole subject. He was denounced by Mr. Follick. Making an impassioned and moving appeal for his Bill, Mr. Follick declared that his leader (Mr. Chuter Ede) had told him he was not interested in the Bill but only wanted to speak long enough to prevent discussion on other Bills.

' "Opponents have twisted the meaning of the Bill to suit their own purposes and my Right Honourable friend (Mr. Chuter Ede) is the biggest sinner of all," exclaimed Mr. Follick.

'The full report can be read in Hansard Vol. 511 No. 63 of the date 27 February 1953.

'After the debate there occurred the most astonishing division ever recorded on a private bill which is generally permitted a free vote, that is without Government direction. The Division List col. 2507 demonstrates that the Government made extraordinary efforts to destroy the Bill. The Government Chief Whip led the way into the No lobby. He was followed by a galaxy of Cabinet Ministers summoned from their offices without having heard a word of the debate. These in turn were supported by Under-secretaries and Junior Whips and Parliamentary Private Secretaries. An analysis shows that of the 53 votes cast against the Bill, 24 were by Ministers or office-holders of some sort. In spite of this determined drive the Bill was triumphantly carried on second reading by 65 votes to 53.

'Standing Committee B met on 24th and 26th March to consider the Bill. The Ministry confidently expected to kill the Bill in Committee. On the contrary, the Bill was passed by the committee after three sensational victories.

'First an amendment was moved to replace the word "shall" with "may." This is the familiar Parliamentary device to take all the "kick" out of a measure. Miss Horsbrugh, supported by Mr. Chuter Ede, advanced the official line that the Bill put compulsion on local authorities. Mr. Pitman counter-argued that authorities were entirely free to do as they liked, but that naturally they would follow the directions of the Bill if they chose to adopt the experiment of teaching to read by simplified spelling. Mr. Ede heard another of his supporters, Mr. Morley, complain that he was guilty of gross misrepresentation. To the alarm of the Ministry the amendment was defeated by 19 votes to 17.

'Secondly, in the second day's debate, when the operative Clause 1 was put to the vote it achieved a tie—15 votes to 15. The Chairman, Mr. Erroll, gave his casting vote in favour of the Clause which was duly passed.

'Thirdly, the official party then tried to stop further proceedings by calling a count. When, at a selected moment, an opponent called the chairman's attention to the lack of a quorum, Miss Horsbrugh, Mr. Pickthorn and their immediate supporters ostentatiously walked out of the committee-room. Great was their chagrin when word was brought to them outside that supporters had come in smartly from other activities to provide just the minimum number required for a quorum despite this manoeuvre. The opponents then gave up the fight. To the astonishment of the Government and many M.P.'s, word went round that the Bill had been reported back to the House.

'The 7th of May was fixed for report and third reading of the Bill in the full House of Commons. But on that date Mr. Follick and Mr. Pitman announced that the Bill would be withdrawn on assurances given by the Minister. Here is the text of a question put by Mr. Follick to the Minister in Parliament and her reply—

Q. To ask the Minister of Education if she will state her policy towards proposals by a competent research organization to investigate possible improvements in the teaching of reading by means of a system of simplified spelling.

A. Any such organization could rely on my interest and goodwill for their proposal as for any proposal designed to investigate possible improvements in this field of education. Such interest and goodwill would not imply any prospect of additional grant. It would be for the organization concerned to secure the willing co-operation of local education authorities, teachers and parents, and these must in my view remain free to decide with what particular forms of research they wish to associate themselves. All concerned in any such researches could rest assured of my good wishes for their work.

'Mr. Follick and Mr. Pitman later issued the following statement—

(i) We are most grateful to the Minister for her attitude towards research into improvement of reading in general, and into this particular aspect of it.

(ii) Now that she has expressed her interest, goodwill and good wishes for such researches, the field is open not only to the two national research bodies (one England and Wales and the other Scotland) but also to the 17 English and Welsh and the four Scottish Universities which have Institutes of Education, any one or more of which now enjoy the most favourable conditions for the conduct of such researches. Any of these research bodies may now point to an encouragement of Ministerial goodwill even more clearly evidenced than ever, to the insistence of the House of Commons that the question of backward reading should receive high-level investigation, and to widespread interest and backing from the public and parents in a matter which affects the nation's most precious asset— the young children.

(iii) We believe that even if the simplification of that which is first presented to the 5-year-old were found to offer no significantly better means of teaching all such children to read fluently, the competitive stimulus of such apparently revolutionary approach will nevertheless promote researches into other new methods and lead to an all-round improvement in existing methods—all of which activities will be potentially most valuable to children.

(iv) We are interested in simplifying spelling not for its own sake— only if such spelling significantly helps the young child to become a fluent reader. If it does not improve the educable ability of all children (and particularly of those who now fail to learn to read) we will (while surprised and disappointed) nevertheless abandon willingly what would then have been shown to offer no important improvement.

(v) When, however (as we believe), simplification for the benefit of the child reader will have been shown by the facts to offer a great improvement in reading ability, millions of young children who would otherwise lose most of the benefit of their school years and lose much in after-life will truly bless this progressive pronouncement by the Minister. Moreover we must not overlook other millions of young children in the English-speaking dominions and countries (where the problem is the same or worse) who will reap the same benefits. Once again English would have taken a decisive lead in the language field and still further consolidated its position as an efficient means of human communication and record.

37

(vi) The Minister in her discussions with us has been keenly aware of and sympathetic with the important issues involved, and has generally—and particularly in this answer—taken the line about improvement of reading and about the use of a new and simplified spelling for which we hoped. We for our part offer a similar spirit of co-operation to the research organizations to which, very properly we consider, the Minister has posed the task and the challenge. The happy ending to the Parliamentary phase will be a happy beginning for the phase of research—actual work in the class-room designed to ascertain facts of a process of learning about which all too little is as yet known.

MONT FOLLICK<br>I. J. PITMAN

'Mr. Follick in a letter to *The Times* some days later wrote that Mr. Gordon Walker and Mr. Morley, as well as Mr. Pitman, advised him to take this course—"to accept the substance of the Minister's assurances and not to go for the shadow." He said it appeared to him that the Prime Minister himself was opposed to the Bill. He believed that the Government could have defeated the Bill on third reading by talking on it beyond 4 o'clock; because it requires 100 M.P.'s to carry a closure motion to bring the debate to a vote, and it is difficult to secure this number of supporters on a Friday when many M.P.'s have already gone to their constituencies.

' "If we had got the Bill," he concluded his letter, "we would not have obtained anything more than the Minister has given us, for the simple reason that we did not ask for much more in the Bill." '

7. The Explanatory Memorandum to the Bill[1] included the following—

'Safeguards are provided to protect the freedom of choice of parent and teacher and the well-being of the child.' Section 1. (5)

8. In the event, it was London University Institute of Education. That leading University Institute was joined by The National Foundation for Educational Research in England and Wales, which latter body thus generously overlooked the threat, apparent only though it had been, which the terms of Parliamentary procedure had forced me (and Follick) to purport to be making. The Directors of these two outstandingly leading Educational Research bodies—Mr. Lionel Elvin and Dr. W. D. Wall—together with Sir William Alexander of the Association of Education Committees, Sir Ronald Gould of the National Union of Teachers and Mr. Walter James, Editor of The Times Educational Supplement, were the five who, at a meeting in the Harcourt Room in the House of Commons, took the initial decision of commitment, and the consequent later ones, to put to the test those theories of Follick and myself which the Minister had thus approved.

9. Extract from letter from George Bernard Shaw to Mr. I. J. Pitman dated 22nd March 1949 (in relation to the first Bill)—

'I think you did unexpectedly well, especially considering the imperviousness of Mr. F. to any sort of political tact. Virtually you broke even with the Government, which was enormously beyond the best that could be hoped. And F. did very well in shewing that practically all the other countries have reformed their spelling. You got a lot across, including the first rate new point about illiterate youths not being able to write love letters, and taking refuge in delinquency.'

10. 'The English language itself is the most simple and the most un-flexioned language that has ever been on earth. The only obstacle to the spread of English is the spelling . . . so that as far as foreigners are concerned, it is one of the most difficult things to learn English and speak it correctly.'

(Dr. M. Follick: *Reform English Spelling*, p. 13)[t]

11. Letter from Bernard Shaw to *Tit-Bits*, 22nd March 1946—[w]

'Everything that Dr. Follick says about our spelling is true; but it was said by Alexander J. Ellis a hundred years ago, and has been repeated again and again by the most eminent phoneticians without producing the smallest effect. The reason is that as so presented the change has seemed enormously expensive and the phonetically spelt texts ridiculous and even sometimes obscene.

'What is needed is a new alphabet of not less than 42 letters, which is the lowest number sufficient to represent all the sounds of spoken English recognizable by a single symbol each. Dr. Follick, by confining himself to 22 letters of the present alphabet, is compelled to represent single sounds by several letters, and has landed himself in such monstrosities as "ei tscheir" to spell "a chair"; 9 letters for 3 sounds! I can write "a chair" 12 times in a minute, and "ei tscheir" only 9 times. The number of minutes in a day is 1,440. In a year 525,600!!!

'To realize the annual difference in favor of a forty-two letter phonetic alphabet as against Dr. Follick's Ootomatik alphabet you must multiply by the number of minutes in the year, the number of people in the world who are continuously writing English words, casting types, manufacturing printing and writing machines, by which the total figure will have become so astronomical that you will realize that the cost of spelling even one sound with two letters has cost us centuries of unnecessary labor. A new British 42 letter alphabet would pay for itself a million times over not only in hours but in moments. When this is grasped, all the useless twaddle about enough and cough and laugh and simplified spelling will be dropped, and the economists and statisticians will be set to work to gather in the orthographic Golconda.

'Work at the figures for yourself. When you do you will waste no more time in repeating and discussing what has been said exhaustively and quite vainly by a century of phoneticians from Ellis to Dr. Follick. The job of designing the new forty-two letter alphabet is one for the British Council; but it may be done in North America or any of the British Dominions.

'Do as much of the propaganda as you can.'

12. Extract from letter from George Bernard Shaw to the Editor of *The Times*, 27th December 1945[w]—

'. . . what I desiderate as a professional writer is an alternative alphabet which will save the millions of hours of manual labour now wasted in a sort of devil worship of Dr. Johnson.'

(Note the words 'an *alternative* alphabet.')

13. Extract from a Public Letter from George Bernard Shaw 'The Author as Manual Laborer' (*sic*): Summer 1944[w]—

'. . . the establishment of a fit British alphabet . . . capable of noting . . . all the sounds of spoken English without having to use more than one letter for each sound, which is impossible with the ancient 26 letter Phoenician alphabet at present in use.'

14. Shaw may well have been right in insisting on a departure from the Roman Alphabet, in order to reduce significantly 'the great disparity' between the convenience and speed of spoken language and the irksomeness and time wasting of written language, as expressed in the words of my late grandfather, Sir Isaac Pitman, in 1842—

'Hitherto, among all nations, there has existed the greatest disparity, in point of facility and dispatch, between these two methods of communication: the former, speech, has always been comparatively rapid, easy and delightful; the latter, writing, tedious, cumbrous, and wearisome. It is most strange that we, who excel our progenitors so far, in science, literature, and commerce, should continue to use a mode of writing, which, by its complexity, obliges the readiest hand to spend at least *six* hours in writing what can be spoken in one. Why do we use a long series of arbitrary marks to represent what the voice utters at a single effort? Why, in short, are not our written signs as simple as our spoken sounds? It cannot be said that this is impracticable.'[b]

15. Extract from the Preface to *The Miraculous Birth of Language*, 1941[x]—

'The new alphabet must be so different from the old that no one could possibly mistake the new spelling for the old.'

Extract from an Open Letter from Bernard Shaw, May 1947[w]—

'Simplified Spelling has been advocated for 100 years without producing the smallest effect. To waste another moment on it seems to me perverse indifference to hard fact. People will not accept a spelling that looks illiterate. To spell English phonetically within the limits of a 26 letter alphabet is impossible. A British alphabet must have at least 44 letters; and though the addition of 19 new letters to Dr. Johnson's stock would distinguish it from illiterate spelling the result would not be Simplified Spelling.'

Extract from a letter from Bernard Shaw to the Editor of *The Times*, 25th September 1906[w]—

'For this very reason, however, the reform cannot be effected by a shortened spelling which is indistinguishable from ordinary wrong spelling. If any man writes me a letter in which through is spelt thru, and above abuv, I shall at once put him down as an illiterate and inconsequent plebeian, no matter what Board or what potentate sanctions his orthography. Really phonetic spelling is quite unmistakeable in this way. No lady or gentleman will ever be persuaded to spell like the late Sir Isaac Pitman, who was a very energetic bookseller and a very bad phonetician; but anybody might spell like Mr. Henry Sweet without compromising himself—indeed with a positive affirmation of having been at Oxford. A practically correct phonetic spelling justified itself at once to the eye as being the spelling of an educated man, whereas the shortenings and so called simplifications suggest nothing but blunders. I therefore respectfully advise the President and the Board to take the bull by the horns without wasting further time, and enlarge the alphabet until our consonants and vowels are for all practical purposes separately represented, and defined by rhyming with words in daily use. We shall then get a word notation which may be strange at first (which does not matter), but which will be neither ludicrous nor apparently ignorant (which does matter very much indeed).

'One other point is of importance. The new letters must be designed by an artist with a fully developed sense of beauty in writing and printing. There must be no apostrophes or diacritical signs to spoil the appearance of the pages of the new type. It is a mistake to suppose that the Bible teaches us the sacredness of pseudo-etymological spelling; but it does teach us the comeliness of a page on which there are no apostrophes and no inverted commas.'


16. Extract from a Public Letter from George Bernard Shaw 'The Author as Manual Laborer' (*sic*): Summer 1944[w]—

'I should strenuously object to have to read, much less write, my own works in a strange script, though I know I should get accustomed to it in a few weeks if I took that trouble.'


17. The learning of a new alphabet is very simple. It is not to be confused with learning a new language—which is a *very* much longer operation. A boy at school who learns Greek characters can learn it in a day and be able to write "brothers and sisters" in the new Greek characters and read them fluently (see p. 12 of The Shaw Alphabet Edition of *Androcles and The Lion*[v]). Those who correspond with the Shaw alphabet have learned to read and write with it with a lack of effort and within a short period of time which has surprised them all.

The use of our present three differing alphabets Bb*b*, Aaα, Ggg, gives us ten such tasks of transfer, or rather adjustment, in the word BAG. These ten transfers we all take in our stride, i.e. BAG, Bag, Bαg, bag, bαg, *baɡ*, bag, bαg, Bag, Bαg.

41

Linguistic transfer, or rather adjustment, is easier than is supposed, both in listening (that is to say in adjusting to the inconsistency of vowel sounds which 'accent' imports), and in reading (that is to say in adjusting to the inconsistencies of pattern which the variety of characters imports).

I was able to learn to 'decipher' (admittedly not to read with skill and consequent fluency) matter employing the alphabet now printed in *Androcles and the Lion*[v] after only four hours, becoming able in that short time virtually to dispense with the transliteration crib, or 'glossary' as Shaw called it. Those long ago who read the new Caroline manuscripts found little difficulty in adjusting themselves to that new and radically different 'a' 'b,' having hitherto been accustomed only to the upper-case letters 'A' 'B'—and even Julius Caesar would have taken little time in relating the new *bellum* to his familiar *BELLVM*, and little longer in acquiring skill to read in that to him quite new alphabet. Writing would have taken him longer.

18. That the extent to which the purpose for which an alphabet is intended affects its forms may be seen by comparing the four specimens below. The first, that of the International Phonetic Alphabet, is intended for the transcription of speech as it varies throughout the world, e.g. because j has three different values in the orthography of French, English, and German *a* choice of value for that character had to be made and as it happens the German was preferred and j used for the sound most frequently represented in English by y, so that yellow and judge become jelou and dʒʌdʒ in I.P.A. Unwonted characters are inevitably much in evidence.

The second, that of Follick, is intended as a spelling reform for English-speaking Europeans in particular and one in which no new characters were to be used. Accordingly the choice of the digraphs (to make good the deficiency of roman characters in relation to English sounds not uttered in Latin) needed to be related to other European orthographies with results necessarily foreign to the English practice, e.g. the ie and the ei in appreciated (aprieshieited) are not only foreign to normal English orthography but ambiguous, since the sound conveyed at the end of the word could be either -iæted or -ɛɛited.

Furthermore while I.P.A. has enough characters for the sounds of English, Follick's system has not. It thus imposes on the learner the disadvantages of all digraphic systems, for example d has one value in *d*he and another in aprieshieiti*d*, h has one value in dhe and two others in *h*uits*h*, etc., etc.

The third is my *i.t.a.* which combines the principle of I.P.A. in having enough characters for the sounds of English, with the principle of leaving those new characters as compatible with the existing orthography as may be possible, in order to avoid unwonted characterizations and spellings and thus unwonted word forms.

The fourth, a "Proposed British Alphabet" is intended for writing more rapidly than with the Roman Alphabet yet to be more easy to learn and more easy to read.

ðis pɔint wil bi wel əpriːʃieitid wen ðis futnout iz stʌdid əz ən igzaːmpl əv ðə greit daivəːdʒəns frəm ðə nɔːməl apiərəns witʃ ðis I.P.A. ælfəbet intrədjuːsiz.

*Follick*

dhis point wil bie aprieshieited huen dhis fuutnout iz studid az an egzampl ov dhu greit daivurjens from dhe normal apierans huitsh dhis I.P.A. alfabet introdiusez.

*i.t.a.*

ʃhis point will bee appreeʃhiæted when ʃhis fœtnœt iʃ studid aʃ an egʃampl ov ʃhe græt dieverjens from ʃhe normal apeerans whiᴄh ʃhis I.P.A. alfabet introdueseʃ.

*Shaw*

ꝺꞮꙄ ꟾꙄꟾ ꟾꞮ ꞮꞮ ꞃꞮꞁꞼꞮꞃꞮꞁꞮ ꞛ⁄ꞟꞟ ꝺꞮꙄ ꞫꝟꞁꞼꝏ ꞮꞫ Ꙅꝟꞛꞟꞟ ꞫꞫ ꞁ ꞮꝳꞫꞩꞩꞮꞃ ꞃ ꝓ ꝳꞫꞛꞮ ꞁꞛꞃꞼꞫꞁꙄ ꞃꞫꞟ ꝓ ꞽꞟꞩꞃꞃ ꞃꞮꞩꝏꙄ ꞛ⁄Ɪꞛ ꝺꞮꙄ I.P.A. ꞽꞃꞃꞮꝟ ꞁꝺꞃꞛꝟꙄꞃꞽ.

The major differences between Follick's system and that of *i.t.a.* are set out below—

| *Follick* | *i.t.a.* |
|---|---|
| dhis | ʃhis |
| wil | will |
| bie | bee |
| aprieshieited | appreeʃhiæted |
| huen | when |
| fuutnout | fœtnœt |
| iz | iʃ |
| az | aʃ |
| egzampl | egʃampl |
| greit | græt |
| daivurjens | dieverjens |
| dhu | ʃhe |
| apierans | appeerans |
| huitsh | whiᴄh |
| introdiusez | introdueseʃ |

19. 'We may get the money . . . to found a Chair . . . in the University of London. It will then be for the University to say how the alphabet should be formed.'

20. The digraphic nature of Follick's representations makes it impossible for him to claim, as he did claim, that all his 23 characters (page 14) have their usual values *and only their usual values*. In contrast, the new characters of *i.t.a.* being characters in their own right [just as *w* is not double *u* (or *double v* as in French) but its own significant unit of representation], do not thus compromise the uniqueness of value of any of the other, non-digraphic, *i.t.a.* characters.

Follick's alphabet 'was finished in the beginning of the year 1914' but not published until much later. (See Follick's 'Author's Note. January 1st 1934'—'The Influence of English.'[c]) I might also have included by way of further comparison the contemporary 'Simplified Spelling' of the Simplified Spelling Society of Great Britain of around that date. A comparison with my Initial Teaching Alphabet seems to be more to the point in 1964, seeing particularly that I deliberately based my (1958) *i.t.a.* upon the work I had done with others on the Simplified Spelling Society alphabet, adopting only those variations in characterization which became possible as improvements as soon as, and because, I had taken the decision not to limit myself to 23 of the 26 letters but to augment the deficiencies by new characters. (See also Note 26.)

Fortunately a comparison between the two systems (and that of Shaw) is made very easy by reason of the close agreement on the nature and number of sounds to be represented (37 Follick, 40 *i.t.a.*, 41 Shaw, including the neutral vowel). The present Simplified Spelling Society's system (and that of The Simpler Spelling Association of America) also recognizes, as does *i.t.a.*, the 40 sounds indicated by number in the right-hand column above the line, on page 27. The Simplified Spelling Society at the date 1914, when Follick wrote the book from which these examples are taken, was deficient, as is Follick, in the additional character necessary to distinguish between the vowels in *pool* and *pull*. Follick and the earlier S.S.S. system represent these two different sounds by but a single character. Follick treats the sound of *oi* digraph originally as two units.

Follick, the S.S.S. and *i.t.a.* do not distinguish the consonant sound of *y* from the vowel sound. Later the British S.S.S. (rather hesitatingly) joined the American S.S.A. in regarding that distinction (e.g. *veri* and *millyon*) as desirable. The Shaw Alphabet makes the distinction. It is, incidentally, interesting that the French name this semi-vowel's character *y*, *i grec*, i.e. the Greek *i*. In words of Greek origin the *y* has indeed the value of *i*, e.g. *synonym*. In both English and French the *y* is used in the place of the Greek upsilon and is pronounced as the vowel in *sin*. Equally in its consonantal form (before a vowel) and in its vowel form (before a consonant) it is used in both (cf. Yolande, Yvonne).

In regard to Follick's use of *u*, it is very odd that he uses that character, sometimes with the value of *uh* as in *but*, *dun* (done), *must*, *suffert*, *up*, sometimes with the value of 'shwa' in *dhu* (the), and sometimes with the value of *wuh* as in *uoz* (was), *huat* (what), *uokt* (walked), *uith* (with), meanwhile using also *uu* for that value (for the shorter vowel) in *stuud* (stood), and also the longer in *ruumert* (rumoured).

44

21. It is noticeable that Follick ignores the fact that a and *a* are radically differing characters: also that he accepts for 14 of his 23 single characters the alternative forms (A B D E F G H I J L M N R T ) as no more differing from their lower-case (and cursive) alternatives than a differs from *a*. It will be noticed that he thus at the outset burdens those learners of English who are not already conditioned to this peculiarity of our Roman alphabet with having to learn a number of alternative characters for one single 'letter' for many of his letters. It is also noticeable that he uses *t* in all past tenses—e.g. *poazt = paused.*

22. Both Follick and *i.t.a.* use *c* as an alternative to *k*, and both use *w*. These characters were not, however, included in the list of what I call 'retentions' on page 118 of 'The Influence of English'[c] but were both used by him in the specimen on page 131.

23. The character here shown in the middle of a, a, ɑ is visually ambivalent between a and ɑ in order to match the corresponding ambivalence in a number of words, e.g. *ask, path, fast, bath,* etc., in which the pronunciation can vary so much in different English-speaking communities. This particular character, being thus ambivalent rather than characteristic, is not counted in the numeration. A total of 44 characters is the normal count of *i.t.a.*'s characterizations.

24. The character ɾ is used in the strong and stressed her, sir, fur and myɾɾ: also in the weak unstressed muᵗher, eliksir, arᵗhur, martyr. (*See also* Note 26.)

25. It will be noticed, as mentioned in Note 21, that the past tense (as in *paused*) has been consistently and thus apparently deliberately represented by a *t* rather than a *d*; also that the plurals of *logs* and *ashes* and the final character in *uos* (was) are an *s* rather than a *z*. These latter are possibly misprints, as is undoubtedly the retention of the *e* in *have* in line 5 of the Follick specimen on page 28. It is to be noticed elsewhere[c] that his *aa* in *Maarz* and *paardun* is not used in the words *part* and *monarks* or incidentally in *after, frans* and *kasks.*

26. The respect which *i.t.a.* pays to the policy of starting at home—and thus to our existing conventions—with the roman alphabet and with our traditional spellings with which we make good its deficiencies—has passed in unbroken descent from Isaac Pitman and A. J. Ellis in their later digraphic alphabets, through Professor Zachrisson, The Simplified Spelling Society (of Britain), and The Simpler Spelling Association (of America).
The Initial Teaching Alphabet was modelled on the alphabet of the S.S.S. of Britain, which in turn was modelled on Isaac Pitman's and those mentioned above. Indeed the digraphs of the S.S.S. became the skeletons upon which the 'augmentations' of *i.t.a.* were designed—save only in the cases of the S.S.S. digraphs aa, dh, and zh, for which the freedom to design and employ an *ad hoc* single character allowed an even closer respect for the traditional form—e.g., ɑ, ᵗh, ȝ, and a no

longer misleading representation in the case of wh. These augmentations were first given aesthetically acceptable form as new characters in a lovely italic script written by the famous calligrapher Alfred Fairbank. The original dated 6 April 1953 still exists, as do a few of the two-page reproductions which were extensively distributed at meetings at those Teacher Training Colleges which were willing to accept a lecture from me.

The alphabet used in the *Times Educational Supplement* article and in the pamphlet 'The Ehrhardt Augmented (40-sound—42-character) Lower-case Roman Alphabet'—Section V—was converted from italic manuscript letters to printer's type letters by The Monotype Corporation as an extension of their existing Ehrhardt alphabet, transliterating the characters drawn by Fairbank into seriffed printer's type in harmony with the existing characters of the Ehrhardt alphabet. Since the introduction of this alphabet (which was first printed in the two first paragraphs of the article 'Learning to Read—A Suggested Experiment,' in *The Times Educational Supplement* of 29th May 1959), there has been only one change—an addition—i.e. *r* (er) was added to make the neutral or central vowel (schwa) more effectively characterized in the single word 'colonel' and whenever spelled in traditional orthography with an r following e, i, u, or y. This made the doubling of the r in *very*, etc., no longer necessary, e.g.—

| | | |
|---|---|---|
| bert | but | beri-beri |
| cur | but | curry |
| sir | but | irak (Iraq) |
| myrr | but | syrup |

and in the four corresponding unstressed forms such as muther, elixir, arthur, and martyr.

27. Extracts from a public letter from George Bernard Shaw, 'The Author as Manual Laborer' [*sic*] Summer 1944[w]—

(a) '. . . Meanwhile the existing generation must have its literature, in the form to which it is accustomed, reading and spelling by visual memory, not by ear.'

(b) '. . . I am ready to make a will . . . introducing a British alphabet . . . always without tampering with the existing alphabet, launching the other in competition with it until one of the two proves the fitter to survive.'

(*See also* Note 12.)

28. This conviction of Shaw's that the 'appeal to the purse' would be the only effective stimulus to adopting a new and more economic medium was stated by him many times. In Clause 35, subsection 1 of his Will[v]: in his letter to *The Times* of December 27th 1945,[w] he was most forthright. In a postcard to me which has become almost famous he wrote:

'I said that the first thing to be provided is an alfabet. But this is not enough. The schools cannot experiment until we provide them with a primer with reading and writing exercises. I am half inclined to draft it myself. Meanwhile write up in letters of gold round your office *England Knows Nothing of Phonetics, Hates Education, But Will Do Anything For Money.*'

Perhaps it was most clearly stated by him in the following—

Extract from a public letter from George Bernard Shaw, 'The Author as Manual Laborer' [*sic*]: Summer 1944[w]—

'When it' [the question of a new alphabet] 'is tackled mathematically the No becomes a clamorous Yes; and the objections are seen to be hot air exhaled by aesthetes who have never counted the prodigious cost of using two letters where one would suffice. To spell Shaw with four letters instead of two, and "though" with six, means to them only a fraction of a second in wasted time. But multiply that fraction by the number of "thoughs" that are printed every day in all the English newspapers in the British Commonwealth and the United States of America—in the books, in the business letters and telegrams, in the private letters, in the military orders; and the fractions of a second suddenly swell into integers of years, of decades, of centuries, costing thousands, tens of thousands and millions. The saving of this colossal waste would pay for the cost of a British alphabet in days, hours, and even minutes. Even the literary upholders of the Phœnician alphabet and its fantastic corruption by the etymological craze would begin to see that Shakespear might have written two or three more plays in the time it took to spell his name with eleven letters instead of seven, "bough" in five instead of two, and so on through much of his vocabulary, though he spelt much more phonetically than Dr. Johnson.

'In my own practice I use the phonetic alphabet of Isaac Pitman, writing without reporters' contractions at my speed of authorship, which averages about 1500 words *per day*. It has saved me a prodigious quantity of manual labor, and can be transcribed on a typewriter by anyone who has spent six weeks in learning the Pitman alphabet; but the time it saves is lost again by the typist, the compositor or linotypist or monotypist, the machinist, the paper makers, and the distributing carriers.'

29. It would be a mistake to regard this great step forward (of multiplication) as tied only to Gutenberg's contribution of movable type. It was only in terms of economy that movable type was an important breakthrough. The same type could be used over and over again. Already by then the main break-through (of multiplication of copies) had been made by others.

Multiplication of copies was in itself doubly important to communication. In the first place it spread knowledge and in the second it conventionalized national speeches and national orthographies. It was the multiplicity of copies which came from the printing press which both made knowledge more widely available and a single convention more widely accepted and employed. It was specifically the King James Bible, read aloud in churches in every parish, at least once every Sunday, which established 'Court English' as the national speech of all England. Read by every literate citizen, it also established the forms from which the national orthography came to be chosen alongside the spoken Court English as the second form of the language for all those provincials who were the natural leaders in their areas of then varying dialect, and of the still more variable orthographies. It thus established a national norm for both speech and print.

There was thereafter a steady movement to conformity in speech, and even more in print. Since the spellings of the King James Bible and their standardization about A.D. 1640 there have been virtually no changes in English spelling. The need for consistency, to spell any given word at least more or less the same way in Genesis and in Exodus, right through to Jude and Revelation, established in the course of time a sanctity as well as a practice in the conventional norm. The public demanded conformity to it from place to place, from book to book, and from year to year. Dr. Johnson's work was thus not the creative one of establishing our spellings but rather of having produced a valuable dictionary, one purpose of which was to enable a standard spelling to be ascertained, so that conformity might be ensured.

30. Sir Thomas Smith's 'New English Alphabet' given in 'Strype's Life of Smith'[a] and his own 'De Recta et Emendata Linguae Anglicae Scriptione,' Paris 1568, is one of the very earliest designs and the first and unique execution of an English alphabet by a Government official at the Court, intended to afford an effectively close relationship between the written and the spoken forms of every English word.

Sir Thomas Smith was Secretary of State in 1548 and again in 1572; he was Ambassador to the French from 1562–1566, and was also author of the important work on the Tudor Constitution 'De Republica Anglorum.'

## BIBLIOGRAPHY

a. *Strype's Life of Smith* (Oxford, at the Clarendon Press, 1820 edition)
b. *Phonography or Writing by Sound*, Isaac Pitman (5th edition, Samuel Bagster & Sons, 15 Paternoster Row, London: 1842)
c. *The Influence of English*, M. Follick (Williams & Norgate, London: 1934)
    (The Author's Note states that the book 'was finished in the beginning of the year 1914.' Although advised 'to bring the book up to date, I did not want to do so, because I thought that this would take the spice out of the work. Some of my forecasts . . . have come about as I foretold in my book they would.')
d. *Hansard*—22nd August 1945 (Her Majesty's Stationery Office, London)
e. *Can English Become a Truly International Language?* M. Follick, M.P. (World Unity Pamphlet No. 1, Jason Press, London: undated, but post-22nd August 1945—possibly January 1946)

f. *Reform English Spelling*, Dr. M. Follick, M.P. (Jason Press, 21 Brownlow Mews, London, W.C.1: October 1946)
g. *Hansard*—11th March 1949 (First Bill) (Her Majesty's Stationery Office, London)
h. *George Bernard Shaw's Letter to Sir James Pitman* after the first Bill—22nd March 1949
j. *Hansard*—6th March 1952—Navy Estimates (Her Majesty's Stationery Office, London)
k. *The Pioneer*—Bulletin of the Simplified Spelling Society: Summer 1952
l. *Simplified Spelling Bill:* 19th November 1952 (Second Bill) (Her Majesty's Stationery Office, London)
m. *Hansard*—27th February 1953 (Her Majesty's Stationery Office, London)
n. *Committee Proceedings of Standing Committee B on the Simplified Spelling Bill* 1953—Second Sitting, 26th March 1953 (Her Majesty's Stationery Office, London)
p. *Hansard*—7th May 1953 (Her Majesty's Stationery Office, London)
q. *The Times*, 12th May 1953, Letter from Dr. Mont Follick.
r. *The Pioneer*—Bulletin of the Simplified Spelling Society: Summer 1953
s. *Weekly Law Reports*—17th May 1957 (The Incorporated Council of Law Reporting for England and Wales, 3 Stone Buildings, Lincoln's Inn, London)
t. *The Times Educational Supplement*, London, 29th May 1959, 'Learning to Read. A Suggested Experiment.'
u. *The Ehrhardt Augmented* (40-*sound*—42-*character*) *Lower-case Roman Alphabet*, I. J. Pitman, M.A., M.P. (39 Parker Street, London, W.C.2: 1959)
v. *Androcles and the Lion* (Shaw Alphabet Edition), George Bernard Shaw (Penguin Books Ltd.: 1962)
w. *On Language: George Bernard Shaw*, edited and annotated by Abraham Tauber, Ph.D. (Philosophical Library, New York: 1963)
x. Shaw's Preface to *The Miraculous Birth of Language*, by Professor R. A. Wilson (Guild Books 1941; J. M. Dent & Sons, Ltd., London, 1942)

# 3

# Regularized English

The only practicable
Solution of the English
Spelling Reform Problem

*by*
A. Wijk

*THE PROBLEM*

FOR hundreds of years it has been generally recognized that
the spelling of the English language is extremely antiquated
and confused, far more so than is the case with any other
living language. Many scholars and laymen have been aware
of the need for reform, and of the enormous benefits it could
entail for the English-speaking peoples as well as for others,
and they have devoted energetic efforts to working out
proposals for a satisfactory new system of orthography.
Special organizations have been founded to deal with the
problem, both in Great Britain and in America, but so far
these attempts have all failed and practically no results at all
of any importance have been achieved. What then have been
the reasons for this failure?

Many will probably think that the conservatism and inertia
of the adult population and their general unwillingness to
accept any changes whatever in their spelling habits are in
themselves enough to account for this failure. But there have
been other and at least equally important reasons as well.
Among them I would particularly point to the fact that it has

proved an exceedingly difficult task to devise a suitable new system of spelling for English—a system which will not only satisfy the demands of philological experts but also stand a reasonable chance of being accepted by the majority of educated people, or at least by a sufficient number, to permit of its being put to the test on a fairly comprehensive scale. As long as there is no such plan worked out in detail, approved by competent experts and accepted by a fairly large number among the educated, we have no real alternative to offer to the existing system of spelling.

In my book, *Regularized English*[1], I have presented a new proposal for a reform of English spelling which ought at least, I think, to stand a better chance of being accepted eventually than the plans that have previously been put forward. I have had some twenty reviews of my book in various philological journals. Nearly all of them have been very favourable. But even so I do not think that my book is very widely known, for the subject of spelling reform is not one that appeals to the public at large. I even fear that to most people it is a highly distasteful subject. I feel almost like apologizing for bringing up this indelicate subject for discussion again.

Let me then state right at the outset that when I began to write my book, about 15 years ago, it was not with the intention to try to bring about an English spelling reform at all costs. That is a project on which the English-speaking peoples will have to make up their minds themselves. My chief purpose was to make a thorough scholarly investigation of the whole problem in order to find out why the various attempts that had been made so far to reform the spelling of English had come to naught, and further to examine what the result would be if we ceased to aim at a more or less perfect 'phonetic' system of spelling and merely replaced the various kinds of irregular spellings in the language by regular ones. I would like to stress that the examination was undertaken

1. Acta Universitatis Stockholmiensis VII, Almqvist & Wiksell, Stockholm, 1959. Also, *Rules of Pronunciation for the English Language* (O.U.P. 1966)

without any preconceived ideas as to the outcome of it. I realized of course that it would be very different from the reform proposals of the Simplified Spelling Society, but I had no very definite idea as to the number and the distribution of the various irregular spellings in the language.

In view of the enormous amount of time and labour which has been expended in trying to find a satisfactory solution of the spelling reform problem, one might ask why no one had ever tried before to investigate this type of solution. For one thing, the investigation proved to be extremely laborious, far more so than I had expected. It took me several years to work through the various sound symbols systematically, to collect and arrange all the exceptional spellings, to discover and formulate the rules for the pronunciation, further to analyse the reform proposals made by the Simplified Spelling Society and the American Simplified Spelling Board, and finally to collect and arrange the statistics concerning the distribution of the irregular spellings. I would like to emphasize that the last-mentioned statistical work could not have been done, if I had not had at my disposal two extremely valuable works on word frequency and word distribution, namely *The Teacher's Word Book of* 30,000 *Words* by Thorndike and Lorge and *The History and Principles of Vocabulary Control* by the Dutchman Hermann Bongers[1].

The results of my investigation were in many respects surprising. They showed among other things that the vast majority of English words, about 90 to 95 per cent of the vocabulary, actually follow certain regular patterns in regard to their spelling and pronunciation. When at first English spelling makes an impression of excessive irregularity, this is largely due to the fact that so many of the irregular words are to be found among the commonest in the language. Thus, among the first thousand of the commonest words, as given in Thorndike and Lorge, no less than 160, i.e. 16 per cent, must without any doubt be considered irregular with regard

1. The former was first published in 1921 with new inlaid additions in 1931 and 1944. The latter appeared in 1947.

to the spelling of either vowel or consonant sounds. And since the first thousand of the commonest words usually make up about 85 per cent of the running words on an average page of prose, as shown by Hermann Bongers in his *History and Principles of Vocabulary Control*, one is easily misled into believing that English spelling is far more irregular than it actually is.

If we examine the second and third thousand of the commonest words, which together with the first make up about 95 per cent of the number of running words on an average page, we shall find that they contain an additional 140 words, i.e. 7 per cent, whose spellings are irregular in one respect or another. From these facts it may be calculated that from 15 to 20 per cent of the words on an average page normally display irregular spellings, a calculation that may easily be confirmed by sampling. In the next following three thousands of the commonest words the percentage remains at about 7 but then falls to about 6 per cent.

In addition to the words which would certainly have to be regarded as displaying irregular spellings, there are on an average page various other types of words which deviate with regard to the pronunciation of certain letters or combinations of letters from the normal sounds of the letters in question, though they cannot be regarded as altogether irregular. If these are included among the irregular spellings, as is not unreasonable, the irregularity would go up to about 10 per cent in the total vocabulary and to about 30 per cent on an average page of prose. Should we wish to regularize the spelling of English, it would therefore be quite sufficient to change the spelling of only 10 per cent of the total vocabulary, and a very large number of these changes would be very slight indeed. About 4 per cent out of the 10 would consist simply in the omission of a final silent *e* or in the change of *s* to *z* in certain positions.

But even a change of only from 5 to 10 per cent of the vocabulary must obviously be regarded as a very violent interference with the language, especially when one considers that such a large number of the commonest words would be affected by it, and it is not to be wondered at that the English-speaking peoples may hesitate to carry out such an operation. The difficulties may, however, to a very large extent be smoothed away if a suitable method of introducing the new system of spelling is adopted. It could in fact be used for as long a period as one would wish simply as a new efficient method for teaching children to read, and it would not be necessary to come to any final decision on the matter until a new generation had grown up who had learnt to appreciate the advantages of the regularized system of spelling.

I said before that the general conservatism of the English-speaking peoples and the force of inertia will by many be regarded as a sufficient reason to explain the failure of the earlier reform proposals. Quite obviously, our feelings are against any change. Spelling is a kind of social habit that we acquire in our childhood and that we do not want to change if it can be avoided. Many have even come to regard the peculiarities and intricacies of English spelling with love and veneration, as something particularly characteristic of English and almost sacred, which it would be a sacrilege to try to change. For many people spelling reform is a subject that they find very hard to think about rationally. But shall we really allow our feelings to get the better of our reason in such an important matter? And should we allow ourselves and our children to be hidebound for all times by an anomalous spelling system which after all has very largely come about simply through the chance decisions of some obscure 16th and 17th century printers?

Another large group of opponents to reform are those who do not think that a reform is necessary. They themselves have perhaps acquired the arts of reading and writing without too much trouble, and they are not aware of the extent of semi-literacy and backwardness in reading amongst English schoolchildren. According to an official investigation into reading ability which was carried out in 1948 by a committee of experts at the request of the then Minister of Education, Mr George Tomlinson, and which was reported in the Ministry of Education Pamphlet No. 18, entitled *Reading Ability*, no less than 30 per cent of all 15-year-olds were classified as backward readers, i.e. as having reading ages 20 per cent below their real ages. Furthermore 1·4 per cent of these were illiterate, and 4·3 per cent semi-literate with reading ages of below 7 years and between 7 and 9 years respectively. Very similar conditions obtain in America, as may be seen from Dr Rudolf Flesch's book, *Why Johnny can't read*, which was published in 1955 and which became a best-seller, evidently because so many parents had found that their children had great difficulties in learning to read.

It is this high percentage of semi-literacy and backwardness in reading among schoolchildren which, from the native speaker's point of view, must be regarded as the chief evidence of the need for reform. For there can be no doubt whatever that this regrettable state of affairs is mainly due to the confused and antiquated spelling system and not, for example, to unsuitable methods of teaching. It should be strongly emphasized, too, that it is not only the backward readers who are exposed to the tortures of the antiquated spelling system. Children of normal ability have of course the same difficulties to contend with and are therefore to a considerable degree bound to be retarded in their progress. It has been estimated that it takes an English-speaking child from one to two years longer to learn to read and write his language than it takes the children of other nations to achieve similar results in their languages. Consequently, if an orthographical system for English could be devised which would be just as simple, regular and logical as those found in most other European languages, it would be possible for all English-speaking schoolchildren to save at least one year's work.

This tremendous saving of time and labour would not be the only important aspect of the question, however. Perhaps even more important would be the fact that such a reform of English orthography would make it possible for English-speaking schoolchildren to learn to read and write in the same way as the children of other nations, i.e. by using and training their sense of logic instead of by training and relying mainly on their eye-memory, learning words by heart without much

55

reference to the sounds of the letters of which they are composed. That the present system of orthography, or rather the apparent lack of system, constitutes a very serious obstacle to the development of the child's reasoning powers is a fact that cannot be denied.

The second main reason which is usually advanced in favour of a reform of English spelling is concerned with the role that the English language plays in foreign countries. To all intents and purposes it must even now be regarded as the principal auxiliary language of the world. But for the great majority of foreigners the language is far too difficult to learn in its present written form. In order to make it more generally acceptable and serviceable as an international auxiliary language it is an indispensable requirement to subject its spelling to a radical and systematic reform.

The need for a common auxiliary language for the whole world has become more urgent every year in the course of the present century. It will therefore not be necessary in this connection to state the various reasons which speak for the creation and propagation of a common second language for all. For a number of reasons English is undoubtedly the living language that is the most suitable to fill this important role. For one thing, English is, though native speakers may perhaps find it hard to believe, a comparatively easy language to learn for foreigners at least as far as the everyday spoken and written forms of it are concerned. This is mainly due to its grammatical structure, which is far simpler than those of most other important languages, and particularly so in comparison with French, German, Russian or Spanish. We need only mention such advantages as the absence of inflection for gender, case and number in the articles, lack of gender in nouns, apart from natural gender, simple ways of forming the plural, the absence of inflection in the adjective, the simple formation of tenses and other verbal forms, etc.

A further obvious advantage of English is its wide-spread distribution in the world of today. Besides being the national language of several of the most important nations of the world today, it is also employed as a second language in most of the newly-emergent Commonwealth countries. And owing to the influential position of the English-speaking peoples and their wide-spread distribution, English is vigorously taught in secondary schools all over the world and is by far the most important language studied in foreign countries. According to the latest calculations about 300 million people now speak English as their native language; to these we should add the large number of foreigners, probably running into ten or possibly even twenty millions who have a satisfactory command of both spoken and written English, and ever so many more millions who are familiar with written English only.

Among the important advantages of English we should finally also emphasize the international character of its vocabulary and its extraordinary capacity for absorbing and developing new linguistic material. These qualities are largely due to the fact that English derives its origin from three principal sources. It is, as we know, mainly a mixture of Germanic, Romance and Latin elements, which makes it eminently suitable for its role as the principal auxiliary language of the world. Owing to its threefold origin, all those who speak or know a modern Germanic or Romance tongue will immediately recognize and understand a large number of words that they come across in the auxiliary language.

But besides all these advantages we also find, as was said before, one great disadvantage, its hopelessly antiquated orthography, which forms a serious obstacle to the general acceptance of English as a universal auxiliary language. In its present written form English simply is not fit for this role.

It should perhaps be pointed out in this connection that the difficulties of English are of a totally different nature for foreigners from what they are for native speakers. For the latter, who pick up the language from hearing it and who already have a fairly large vocabulary when they begin to learn to read and write it, the chief difficulties lie in learning to recognize words and to write them correctly, whereas they have little trouble in learning to pronounce them. For foreigners, on the other hand, who have already learnt to

57

read their own native language when they start learning English, reading and writing do not in themselves present any new problems. For them it is the pronunciation of all the words that they come across in written English that constitutes the major difficulty, besides the acquisition of a sufficient vocabulary. On account of the large number of irregular spellings among the commonest words in the language it is impossible to lay down any rules for the connection between spelling and pronunciation in English which would be useful to them, in the earlier stages of their study. They then have to learn each word that they come across by itself, either from a teacher or with the help of some kind of phonetic transcription. It goes without saying that a reform of English spelling which would eliminate the vast majority of irregular spellings and thus make it possible to infer the pronunciation from the spelling, would enormously facilitate the learning of the language for all foreign students, while at the same time it would make it very much easier for English-speaking children to learn to read and write their language.

The problem of devising a suitable new system of orthography for English may perhaps at first seem to be a comparatively easy one; but anyone who endeavours to penetrate more deeply into the question will soon find that it is fraught with formidable difficulties. The mere fact that the numerous attempts which have been made to solve it, both by eminent individual scholars and by societies specially founded for the purpose, have all failed to produce an acceptable solution, is in itself a sufficient indication of the intricate nature of the problem.

The solution that immediately presents itself to the mind is to create a new phonetic alphabet for English by selecting the most suitable symbol for each of its forty odd speech sounds. These symbols are then to be used as consistently as possible for the spelling of all words. Among the best and most carefully thought out systems of this kind are undoubtedly the one proposed around 1930 by the Swedish scholar Professor R. E. Zachrisson, called *Anglic* or *English in Easy Spelling*, and the one devised by the Simplified Spelling

Society, who in 1940 brought out their publication *New Spelling*, based on a careful statistical investigation of the present spelling. Actually these two systems agree pretty closely with one another, particularly with regard to the treatment of the stressed vowels and the consonants. Thus both of them introduce the same special new symbols for the so-called long sounds of the five simple vowels, namely *ae*, *ee*, *ie*, *oe* and *ue*. These symbols are to be used in all words in which the speech sounds in question are found, whether now represented by the simple vowels or by combinations of vowel letters or by combinations of vowel letters with certain consonants. In view of the frequent occurrence of these sounds it is obvious that this feature is bound to cause an extremely violent break in continuity between the traditional and the suggested new system of spelling. Other features which were common to *New Spelling* and *Anglic* and which would contribute to causing similar violent breaks in continuity were the regular replacing of *c* and *q* by *k* when they stood for the *k*-sound, of *c* by *s* whenever it stood for the voiceless *s*-sound, and of *g* and *j* when it represented the regular *j*-sound. A brief specimen of the Simplified Spelling Society's *New Spelling* follows below:

Objekshonz to a Chaenj in dhe Prezent Speling.

We instinktivly shrink from eny chaenj in whot iz familyar; and whot kan be mor familyar dhan dhe form ov wurdz dhat we hav seen and riten mor tiemz dhan we kan posibly estimaet? We taek up a book printed in Amerika, and *honor* and *center* jar upon us every tiem we kum akros dhem; nae, eeven to see *forever* in plaes ov *for ever* atrakts our atenshon in an unplezant wae. But dheez ar iesolaeted kaesez; think ov dhe meny wurdz dhat wood hav to be chaenjd if eny real impruuvment wer to rezult. At dhe furst glaans a pasej in eny reformd speling looks 'kweer' or 'ugly'. Dhis objekshon iz aulwaez dhe furst to be maed; it iz purfektly natueral; it iz dhe hardest to remuuv. Indeed, its efekt iz not weekend until dhe nue speling iz noe longger nue, until it haz been seen ofen enuf to be familyar.

In spite of extensive propaganda this proposal for a

reformed spelling has never succeeded in arousing any wide-spread interest among the general public, which is not particularly surprising in view of the fact that it entails a complete transformation in the appearance of the language. There is nothing very wrong with the system as such, but when we come to examine it more closely, we shall find that it leads to a change in spelling in 90 per cent or more of the vocabulary. The same applies to all similar attempts to create a phonetic alphabet for English to replace the present spelling system.

## THE PROPOSED SOLUTION.

Since the phonetic principle leads to such extensive changes in the spelling and since a solution of this kind obviously does not stand the slightest chance of ever being accepted, we shall have to examine whether there may not be other methods of achieving a systematic reform. The only alternative that offers the possibility of a general revision of the whole spelling system is to start out instead from the various existing symbols and try to determine how they should best be used in a reformed orthography. What we have to do, exactly, is first to examine in detail how these symbols are now used, and then to decide which uses may conveniently be retained and which should be discarded. Generally speaking, all the regular, i.e. the most frequent, uses of the various sound symbols should be preserved, whereas all irregular spellings should be discarded and replaced by regular ones. If in the application of these general rules we give up the idea of strict adherence to the phonetic principle and allow, on the one hand, certain symbols to represent more than one sound, and, on the other, certain sounds to be represented by more than one symbol, when this can be done without causing undue confusion, we shall find that it becomes possible to work out a spelling system for English which on the whole may be said to satisfy all reasonable requirements with regard to order and regularity and which will enable us to establish definite rules of pronunciation for the English language.

Since the fundamental idea of this 'new' system of spelling is to preserve *all* the various sound symbols of the present orthography in their *regular*, i.e. in their most frequent usage or usages, it may suitably be called *Regularized Inglish*. On a closer examination it will be found that the principles of Regularized Inglish enable us to retain the present spelling in over 90 per cent of the vocabulary, whereas the *New Spelling* of the Simplified Spelling Society only preserves it in about 10 per cent or less of the words. The following three specimens will give a general impression of the proposed new spelling. The first specimen is a rendering of the same text as was given in *New Spelling* above.

1. Objections to a Chainge in the Prezent Spelling.

We instinctivly shrink from eny chainge in whot iz familiar; and whot can be more familiar than the form ov wurds that we hav seen and written more times than we can possibly estimate? We take up a book printed in America, and *honor* and *center* jar upon us every time we cum across them; nay, even to see *forever* in place ov *for ever* attracts our attention in an unplezant way. But theze ar isolated cases; think ov the meny wurds that wood hav to be chainged if eny real improovement wer to rezult. At the first glaance a passage in eny reformd spelling looks 'queer' and 'ugly'. This objection iz aulwayz the first to be made; it iz perfectly natural; it iz the hardest to remoove. Indeed, its effect iz not weakend until the new spelling iz no longer new, until it haz been seen offen enuff to be familiar.

2. By the adoption ov such a system ov spelling az Regularized Inglish it wood be possible to lay down definit rules ov pronunciation for the Inglish language, which wood make it considerably eazier for children to lern to read and write. In aul probability it wood lead to a saving ov at least wun year's wurk for aul scoolechildren. It wood aulso contribute very largely towordz abolition ov the existing amount ov illiteracy and backwardness in reading. Finally it wood remoove the principal obstacle that prevents Inglish from becumming a truly international language.

3. From *Hamlet*, Act III, Scene 1.

> To be, or not to be: that iz the question:
> Whedher 'tiz nobler in the minde to suffer
> The slings and arroes ov outrageous fortune,
> Or to take arms against a sea ov trubbles,
> And by oppozing end them? To die; to sleep;
> No more; and by a sleep to say we end
> The hart-ake and the thouzand natural shocks
> That flesh iz eir to, 'tiz a consummation
> Devoutly to be wisht. To die, to sleep;
> To sleep! perchaance to dream; ie, thare'z the rub;
> For in that sleep ov deth whot dreams may cum,
> When we hav shuffled off this mortal coil,
> Must giv us pauze: thare'z the respect
> That makes calamity ov so long life.

Before passing on to a somewhat more detailed discussion of the application of the above-mentioned principles, it may be appropriate to give a brief survey of the number of speech sounds or phonemes that are found in present-day Standard English and of the number of symbols that are normally used to represent them in the written form of the language. It would seem that many people have exaggerated ideas as to the number of symbols that are used in ordinary English spelling. We find in spoken Standard English 46 different speech sounds, 21 vowels and diphthongs and 25 consonants. In the written form of the language the 21 vowels and diphthongs are normally represented by 60 different symbols and the 25 consonant sounds by 44 symbols, as given in the lists below:

Symbols of simple vowels and diphthongs: a, e, i, y, o, u; ar, er, ir, yr, or, ur; aa, ae, æ, ai, ay, au, aw, ea, ee, ei, ey, eu, ew, ie, ye, oa, oe, œ, oi, oy, oo, ou, ow, ue, ui, uy; aer, air, ayr, ear, eer, eir, eyr, eur, ew(e)r, iar, ier, yer, oar, oor, our, ow(e)r, uer; igh, aigh, augh, eigh, ough=60

Symbols of consonant sounds: b, c, ch, d, dg, f, g, gh, gn, gu, h, j, k, l, m, n, ng, p, ph, q, qu, r, s, sc, sch, sh, si, ssi, sci, ti, ci, ce, t, tch, th, u, v, w, wh, x, xc, y, z, zi=44

If we add up the vowel and consonant symbols, we find that the 46 sounds of the spoken language are normally represented by 102 symbols in the written language (60 plus 44 minus 2, since *u* and *y* stand for both vowel and consonant sounds). If double consonants are added, we get 15 more symbols:

bb, cc, dd, ff, gg, ck or cq (instead of 'kk'), ll, mm, nn, pp, rr, ss, tt, vv, zz.

When it is sometimes said that there are more than 250 different symbols (or even many more) for the 46 speech sounds, this is only due to a peculiar way of counting, which we need hardly enter into in this connection.

In the second and larger part of my book I have subjected each one of the 102 symbols that are used to represent the 46 speech sounds of the language, to a thorough, systematic examination in order to find out how they could best be employed in a reformed spelling system, in case it should prove desirable and possible to carry out such a reform. I have first established what is the normal pronunciation for each one of the symbols and have then tried to give as complete an account as possible of the various deviations that occur. Since there can be no question of going through the 102 symbols here, I shall have to content myself with a discussion of the principles I have applied and with giving a number of examples of the way the problems have been dealt with.

Among the numerous difficulties that confront the would-be spelling reformer in his attempt to devise a satisfactory new system of spelling, the greatest is undoubtedly the problem of how to deal with the five simple vowels, which, as we know, normally have two principal pronunciations in stressed syllables, a so-called short one and a so-called long one. Actually the main difference between them is now one of quality rather than of length. Since most spelling reformers were anxious to establish a consistent 'phonetic' spelling for English, it seemed essential to them to distinguish between the two pronunciations by using different symbols for them, and since the short pronunciation is by far the commoner one, this value was retained for the present symbols, whereas new symbols were selected to represent the long pronunciation, thus for example the *ae, ee, ie, oe, ue* of the Simplified Spelling Society's *New Spelling* or Professor Zachrisson's *Anglic*. We should recall in this connection that the long sounds of the simple vowels are also frequently represented by various digraphs in the present orthography. Since, in a phonetic system of spelling, these digraphs too would have to be replaced by the new symbols (if not identical with them), it is not surprising that the total effect of the proposed changes was such as to cause a complete transformation in the appearance of the language.

One must seriously question, however, whether it is really essential to create new symbols for the long sounds of the simple vowels in order to distinguish their two principal pronunciations. That will depend on whether the present spelling may be said to provide adequate guidance as to the pronunciation or not. If the distribution of the short and the long sounds is more or less arbitrary, so that we can never tell from the spelling whether to use one pronunciation or the other, the existing spelling system cannot be regarded as satisfactory. Such is by no means the case, however. For the vast majority of the words which contain the five simple vowels in stressed syllables, the present spelling offers on the whole sufficient guidance as to the pronunciation when supplemented by certain not very complicated rules. Unfortunately these rules are not very widely known, and they have often been wrongly or inappropriately formulated.

Thus, in many books dealing with this subject, it is stated that the long and the short pronunciation of the simple vowels in stressed syllables depends in principle on whether the syllables are open or closed, i.e. whether they end in a vowel or in a consonant. This might lead one to suppose that it would normally be possible to infer the pronunciation of the vowels by learning the rules for the division of words into syllables. We might rather say that the contrary is the case, since the correct division of words generally depends on whether the preceding vowel has its short or its long pronunciation. When the vowel is short, words are divided *after* the following consonant, thus for example 'lav-ish, vic-ar, com-ic, cap-ital, vet-eran, prob-able', etc. In these words the first syllable is consequently to be looked upon as closed and not as open, as it is sometimes said to be. When the preceding vowel is long, words are usually divided *before* the following consonant, thus for example in 'ma-jor, no-tice, fa-ther, mu-sic, sa-cred, li-brary', etc. In the case of inflected forms of words ending in a single consonant plus silent *e*, words such as 'make fine, hope',—which words cannot themselves be divided and which should properly be regarded as closed syllables, since they end in a consonant in their pronunciation—the consonant usually goes with the stem of the word, thus for example 'mak-ing, debat-ed, lat-er', etc. We may note that the division of words is nowadays indicated in many dictionaries, among others in the well-known *The Advanced Learner's Dictionary of Current English* and in the *American College Dictionary*.

From this discussion it is clear that the division of words into closed and open syllables cannot be considered an entirely suitable basis in setting up rules for the distribution of the short and long pronunciations of the simple vowels. Instead words should be divided into different categories according to, on the one hand, the position of the vowels in words, whether before consonants or before vowels or in final position, and, on the other hand, according to the position of the main accent, which it is necessary to know to be able to pronounce them correctly. The problem of the correct position of the accent is sometimes held to offer one of the greatest difficulties of English pronunciation, but from the statistical point of view the placing of the accent does not cause any great difficulty for the vast majority of words, and here, too, it is possible to set up a number of very helpful rules.

Starting out from the various factors just referred to, I have managed to set up eight categories of words in which we normally find the short pronunciation, and eight categories in

65

which we find the long one. Together they probably cover well over 95 per cent of all the words which contain simple vowels in stressed syllables. It may of course sound quite complicated to have no less than eight categories of words for each of the two main types of pronunciation, but it should be pointed out that for children who are beginning to learn to read, it would for a long time be fully sufficient to learn only three or four of these categories. As far as the acquisition of the art of reading is concerned, they may in fact never need to learn any more categories at all. The three principal rules for the distribution of the short and long sounds run as follows:

No. 1. The short sound is normally used in all words of one syllable which end in one or more consonants and in such words of two or more syllables as are stressed on the last syllable and end in one or more consonants. Examples: glad, leg, thing, fond, cup, attack, attempt, distinct, etc.

No. 2. The short sound is used in all words of two or more syllables in which the main stress falls on a syllable before the last and in which the stressed vowel is followed by two or more consonant-letters. Examples: candy, fellow, picture, hospital, hunger, etc.

No. 3. The long sound is normally used in all words in which the simple vowel is followed by a single consonant plus silent *e*. Examples: make, these, fine, hole, tune, debate, extreme, polite, etc.

The words in ordinary English which form exceptions to these general rules, will have to be changed in their spellings in Regularized Inglish, just as they will have to be changed in any transitional spelling system that may be used for helping children to learn to read. Thus for example *a* will be replaced by *aa* in such words as 'half, fast, dance', by *au* in such words as 'all, salt, talk', by *o* in 'want, wash, watch', by *e* in 'any, many', etc., *e* will be replaced by *i* in 'English' and 'pretty', *o* by *u* in 'come, among, love', *u* by *oo* in 'full, push, put', etc. The final silent *e* will have to be dropped in such words as 'have, give, live' but will be added after two consonants in such words as 'bind, find, both, most, post', etc., after the analogy of 'haste, paste, taste'.

As for the remaining rules for the distribution of the short and long pronunciation, we should note that they are very important for understanding the structure and the degree of regularity of the English spelling system, even though they are not essential to know for children who are learning to read. I cannot go through all of them here, but I may mention two or three of them which comprise very extensive categories of words. Thus we find the short sound with great regularity in words in which the stressed syllable is followed by two or three syllables, even when the simple vowel is only followed by a single consonant, for example in such words as 'animal, enemy, criminal, colony, vocabulary, decorative, solitary', etc. The rule certainly applies to at least 95 and possibly even to as many as 98 per cent of the words of the type in question. We have further an extremely large group of words which end in an unstressed syllable containing any one of certain vowel combinations, *ia*, *io*, *iou*, *iu*; or *ea*, *eo*, *eou*, *eu* or *ie*, words such as 'politician, delicious, official, religion, familiar; nation, devotion, legion, social, crucial, facetious, patient, copious, dubious, radio, polio, studio', etc. In non-final syllables of words of this kind *i* is always short without a single exception, whereas the other four simple vowels are nearly always long, with very few exceptions.

I have so far only discussed words in which the simple vowels are not followed by the letter *r*. When they occur in the combinations *ar*, *er*, *ir*, *or*, *ur*, there are special rules for the pronunciation which are extremely reliable. The exceptions are so few that they can easily be learnt by heart, anyway by foreign students. For each of the four combinations *ar*, *er*, *ir*, *ur* we generally find, in both British and American English, three regular pronunciations in stressed syllables, two long ones and one short, whereas the fifth combination, *or*, has only two principal pronunciations, one long and one short. To illustrate the rules for the distribution of the three pronunciations we may select the combination *ar*.

1. The first long pronunciation, [aː],[1] is only found in final or preconsonantal position and in derivatives of words in which it occurs in these positions, for example in 'car, far, farm, hard, market', etc. The only exception is the word 'scarce, scarcely' and words with *ar* after *w*, *qu*, such as 'war, warm, quarter'. In Regularized Inglish the spelling of 'scarce' would have to be changed to 'scairce' and after *w*, *qu*, *a* would be replaced by *o* or by *au*.

2. The second long pronunciation, |ɛə|, is only found before a final silent *e* or before a pronounced vowel-letter, in such words as 'care, dare, parent, vary', etc. The only exception is the auxiliary 'are', in which the *e* would have to be dropped, and certain loanwords, such as 'safari, Sahara', etc., which had better be left unchanged.

3. The short pronunciation, which is simply the regular short sound plus *r*, is only found before a pronounced vowel-letter or when *r* is written double, thus in words such as 'baron, charity, carrot, marry', etc. The only exceptions are after *w*, *qu*, as in 'warrior, quarrel', in which *a* would have to be changed to *o* in Regularized Inglish.

In the case of the combination *er* there are only five important words whose spellings would need changing in Regularized Inglish, 'clerk' and 'sergeant', in which *er* should be replaced by *ar*, further 'there, where', which would instead be written *thare, whare*, and finally the preterite 'were', in which the final *e* should be dropped.

In the case of *ir* we find only one irregular word in the language, 'iron', in which the *r* is not pronounced before a vowel, as it usually is. It ought to come after the *o* instead of before.

In the case of *or* there are about a dozen words whose spellings would need to be changed in Regularized Inglish, namely such words as 'word, world, work, worse, worst, worth' in which *or* should be replaced by *ur*, and further the three words 'borough, thorough, worry', in which *or* should be replaced by *urr*.

1. Pronunciation is indicated by means of I.P.A.-transcription.

Finally we have the combination *ur*, for which there is only one word with an irregular pronunciation, 'bury, burial', in which *ur* should be replaced by *er* (or possibly by *err*).

Having dealt with the various problems connected with the regularization of the use of the five simple vowels, I will now pass on to a brief discussion of the so-called digraphs, i.e. the combinations of two vowel letters that are used to represent some of the speech sounds or phonemes of which the language is made up, whether pure vowel sounds or diphthongs. We find 32 combinations of this kind, but only 22 of them are of such frequent occurrence that they may be said to play an important part in the English spelling system. We should further note that twelve of them form pairs, the members of which always normally stand for the same sound: *ai*, *ay*; *ei*, *ey*; *oi*, *oy*; *au*, *aw*; *eu*, *ew*; and *ou*, *ow*. If we examine the use of the digraphs in the present orthography, we shall find that in nearly every case one particular usage is the predominant one, whereas other pronunciations that are found for them, must be regarded as exceptional. Under such circumstances the obvious course to follow, if one wishes to regularize the spelling, is to restrict each particular symbol to denote one sound only, in accordance with the predominant usage, and to change the spellings of those words which show deviations from this pronunciation into one of the regular spellings for the sound in question. Let us by way of illustration select a few of these digraphs and examine what will happen if this procedure is followed.

For the digraphs *ai*, *ay* the predominant usage in ordinary English is 'the long sound' of *a*, as found for instance in 'maid, fail, rain, day, pay'. For Regularized Inglish these symbols should therefore be restricted to stand for this sound only, except in front of *r*, where they should instead represent the sound we have in such words as 'air, fair, pair'. There are only seven important words in which we find deviations from these pronunciations. We have the short sound of *a* in 'plaid, plait', the short sound of *e* in 'says, said', the long sound of *e* in 'quay', and the long sound of *i* in 'aisle, aye'. For these words I have consequently suggested that the spellings should be changed in Regularized Inglish, into *a* in 'plad, plat', into *e* in 'sez, sed', into *kea* for 'quay' and *yle, ie* for 'aisle, aye'. The spelling *kea* is because the other word 'key' will have to be changed into *kee*, since *ey* (as well as ei) always stands for the sound |ei| in Regularized Inglish. *yle* for 'aisle' is because of the other word 'isle' (island), in which *s* will have to be dropped. Some of these changes may seem shocking, but they are essential, if you want to make it easy for children to learn to read. As for words such as 'aisle' and 'aye', they need of course never be used at all in reading schemes for beginners, but it is important to know how they should be dealt with, if the need should arise.

Passing on to the digraph *ea* we find somewhat more complicated conditions. The predominant usage for *ea* in present-day English is the long *e*-sound, as found for instance in 'beat, meat, each, leave, mean', etc. For Regularized Inglish it will therefore be appropriate to restrict the use of *ea* to denote this sound only. Besides the words with the long *e*-sound we find in the present orthography a fair number of words in which the symbol *ea* is pronounced as *e* short, as in 'bread, death, health, measure, weather', etc. (some 60 to 70 words in all). In all these the digraph *ea* should be replaced by *e* in Regularized Inglish. We further find a few words in which *ea* is pronounced |ei|, namely in 'great, break, steak' and 'yea'. For the first three I have suggested that *ea* should be replaced by *ei*, which in Regularized Inglish always stands for the sound |ei|. For 'yea' I have suggested a change of spelling to 'yay' on account of its opposite 'nay'.

When the digraph *ea* occurs before *r*, the combination *ear* represents no less than four different pronunciations in the present orthography. Since the one which most nearly agrees with the regular sound of *ea* is that found in such words as 'clear, dear, ear, fear', etc., and since this is also the commonest pronunciation, it will be convenient to restrict *ear* to denote this particular sound in Regularized Inglish. When the combination *ear* represents other sounds in the present orthography, the spelling will therefore have to be changed. Thus it is suggested that *ear* should be replaced by *air* in the four words 'bear (verb), tear, wear, swear'. For the nouns 'bear, pear' it is suggested that *ear* should be replaced by *ayr* instead, in order to distinguish them from the verb 'to *bair*' (bear) and the adjective 'bare' and from 'pair' and 'pare' respectively.—The combination *ear* further occurs in 14 words before a following consonant with the sound |ə:|, as in 'early, earn, earnest, earth', etc. For these words it is suggested that *ear* should be replaced by *er*. Finally there are three words, in which *ear* is pronounced [a:], namely 'heart, hearth, hearken'. For these it is suggested that *ear* should be replaced by *ar*.

On the same lines as has been indicated for the symbols *ai, ay, air* and *ea, ear* I have regularized the usage of most of the remaining digraphs in the proposed reformed spelling. The total number of the suggested spelling changes, for stressed and unstressed vowels as well as for the consonants, amounts to only about 10 per cent of the total vocabulary.

For two of the digraphs, for *ie* and *oo*, I have had to allow two pronunciations in Regularized Inglish, for the following reasons.

The digraph *ie* has two principal pronunciations in ordinary English, 'the long sound' of *e*, as in 'belief, believe, chief, field, thief', etc., and the "long sound" of *i*, as in 'die, dies, died, cries, cried', etc. The two pronunciations are always kept strictly apart. The former only occurs *within* words and the latter only *at the end* of words or in inflected forms. For this reason and because they are both common in ordinary English, it will be convenient to retain them in Regularized Inglish. In two words only, 'sieve' and 'friend', do we find abnormal pronunciations. The spellings of these will therefore have to be changed to *siv* and *frend* respectively in Regularized Inglish.

Also for the digraph *oo* we find two principal pronunciations in ordinary English, which may be called the long and the short *oo*-sound respectively. The long sound, as found in 'boot, cool, choose, moon, tooth', etc., is by far the commoner one, and from this point of view it would have been desirable to restrict the use of *oo* to denote this sound only. The short sound occurs regularly before *k* in such words as 'book, cook, look, took', etc., but otherwise only in a comparatively small number of words, such as 'foot, good, stood, wood, wool', etc. Unfortunately there is no other symbol than *oo* that can conveniently be used to render the short sound, so *oo* will have to serve for both. Since the two sounds are closely alike in quality, I do not think that this will cause any difficulty whatever from the native speaker's point of view. However, in order to obviate this difficulty as far as possible, I have suggested that in Regularized Inglish a final silent *e* should be added, in conformity with the usage for the simple vowels, to all those words in which the long sound is followed by a final single consonant or by two final consonants in the present orthography. We may note that such a silent *e* is found in many words in the present spelling, for instance in 'goose, loose, choose, groove, soothe', etc.

The many variant pronunciations that are found for nearly all the digraphs in the present orthography constitute one of the greatest difficulties of the language, both for native speakers when they are learning to read, and for foreigners who want to acquire a correct pronunciation. It is therefore easy to understand what a tremendous difference it will make, when in Regularized Inglish the digraphs are restricted in their usage, so that it becomes possible to lay down definite rules for their pronunciation.

To round off my account of the proposed new spelling system I should finally also discuss how the various principles which have been laid down for a regularization of the spelling should be applied to the vowels and diphthongs of unstressed syllables and to the consonants. Since the *most* essential aim in a reform of the spelling must be to make it easier to learn to *read* rather than to learn to *write* correctly, and since, on the whole, the existing spelling system does not present any very great difficulties from this point of view, it follows that only comparatively slight changes are required in order to provide adequate guidance as to the pronunciation. In these circumstances I think we may perhaps omit a discussion of the unstressed vowels and the consonants.

Having dealt with the principles for the regularization of the spelling and having given a number of examples of the way it has been carried out for some of the 104 symbols which are used to represent the 46 English speech sounds, it still remains for me to indicate what effect the application of the various rules will have in practice and to what extent the present spelling will be changed if the new system is adopted. In the six appendices to my book I have made a detailed statistical investigation of these questions based on an analysis of a number of parallel texts in Regularized Inglish and in The Simplified Spelling Society's *New Spelling* and on a study of the changes in spelling which will have to be made among the 10,000 commonest words as given in Thorndike and Lorge. I can here only give a brief summary of the most important results.

From the analysis of the texts it appears that about 30 per cent of the words on an average page normally display changes in spelling in Regularized Inglish, whereas in the Simplified Spelling Society's *New Spelling* the changes amount to about 70 per cent. Out of the 30 per cent of changed spellings in Regularized Inglish more than two thirds are covered by just a few dozen words of high frequency, such as 'ov, iz, hav, ar, thare, whot, widh, az, eny, meny, aul', etc. From this we may conclude that the number of the remaining words whose spellings have been changed, amounts to less than 10 per cent of the total number of running words. Since the percentage of change within the total vocabulary will hardly be affected at all by those changes that are found in 40 or 50 or even 100 words of extremely high frequency, we have every reason to believe that for Regularized Inglish the number of suggested changes will amount to less than 10 per cent of the total vocabulary.

From a similar examination of the specimen texts for the Simplified Spelling Society's *New Spelling* we may infer that here the number of suggested changes amounts to at least 90 per cent of the total vocabulary, which explains why it has never aroused any wide-spread interest.

We arrive at the same results when we study the number of

irregular spellings that occur among the 10,000 commonest words in the language. As is to be expected, the largest number of them is to be found among the 3,000 commonest words where they amount to 21 per cent. In the next following 3,000 words the percentage falls to 13 and in the next following 4,000 words to 10. Since it is the last 4,000 out of the 10,000 commonest words that are most typical of the vocabulary in its entirety, we here find it confirmed that the number of words which display irregularities as regards spelling or pronunciation only amounts to about 10 per cent of the vocabulary.

## IMPLEMENTATION.

I said earlier in this lecture that my chief intention when I started writing my book was to examine what the result would have been if, instead of aiming at a completely phonetic system of spelling, one had contented oneself with abolishing the irregular spellings in the language and replacing them by regular ones. This purpose implied that I had to carry out my investigation in all its numerous details, with the constant aim of devising a satisfactory new system of orthography for English. It will not be enough, however, merely to devise a satisfactory new system of orthography. Since the question of spelling reform is one which intimately concerns all classes of society, it will be equally essential to devise a method for overcoming the resistance to spelling reform among the adult population in general. Let us then assume for the moment that we would like to try to bring about such a reform. How should we go about it?

The best way to prepare the ground for a future reform will undoubtedly be to start experiments in schools on a fairly extensive scale in order to show that English reading and writing can be taught far more easily, rapidly and successfully than is now the case by first teaching it in the form of Regularized Inglish and transferring afterwards, say after a year or so, to ordinary English. Since the spelling of Regularized Inglish is almost a hundred per cent regular in the application of its rules of pronunciation, it will be considerably easier to learn to read and write than ordinary English. Very probably all children of normal intelligence will learn to read it tolerably well in about a year. But once children have learnt to read Regularized Inglish, they will immediately be able to read ordinary English as well, in spite of the many irregularities of the latter spelling. For once a child has learnt to read according to one system of orthography, there is no great difficulty about reading according to another which employs the same or similar characters. Thus, for example, all foreign children who have learnt to read their own language and who belong to nations that use the Roman alphabet, will be able to read most English words at first sight, though of course without the proper pronunciation and without understanding them. This is what one might perhaps call an example of 'instant reading'.

Since the spelling of Regularized Inglish agrees in over 90 per cent of the words with that of ordinary English, and since the new spelling retains nearly all the *regular* features of traditional English, children would, if this method of teaching were adopted, have a chance to make themselves thoroughly familiar with all these regular features of the language before starting to learn all the exceptions. This will undoubtedly prove to be a better and more gratifying way of learning to read than the methods which have been in general use so far, and which either aim at teaching children each regularly or irregularly pronounced word as a whole, the so-called 'whole word method', or else, and far more commonly, have been based on a combination of 'phonics', i.e. the old time-honoured method of sounding out the various letters, and the so-called 'new' whole word method, which was of course always employed in the case of words with anomalous spellings. On account of the prevailing methods of teaching reading it seems highly probable that most English-speaking children now grow up under the entirely false impression that there are no reliable rules concerning the relations between spelling and pronunciation in their language.

If the method for teaching reading which I have just

75

indicated, is adopted for a sufficiently long transitional period, say for thirty or forty years, it is perhaps not unlikely that the new generation of adults which will have grown up by then, will be prepared to take the necessary steps to carry out a reform. On the other hand there is nothing in the plan itself that must of necessity lead to a reform. It could very well be used simply as a new, more efficient method for teaching reading. Since the results of the methods that are now in general use must undoubtedly be regarded as extremely unsatisfactory, and since for my own part I am thoroughly convinced that the only way to bring about any essential improvement in this matter, is to employ a transitional spelling system which is regular in character, I would suggest that experiments of this kind should be carried out on an extensive scale. There can in my opinion be no more important object for research for any educational institution in Great Britain and America.

Before such experiments can be carried out, it will be necessary to prepare a suitable textbook, or perhaps rather a series of short textbooks. These should be carefully graded and proceed at a very slow pace from simple to more difficult things. It is important, too, that they should be attractive in appearance and amply illustrated like ordinary readers for beginners. As for the general plan to be followed in such textbooks I will not take it up for discussion now, but it would not be very different from the course that is usually followed in reading schemes for beginners.

## COMPARISON BETWEEN I.T.A. AND REGULARIZED ENGLISH.

Since it was one of the purposes of my book to try to devise a satisfactory new system of spelling for English, I have so far only had occasion to draw comparisons with certain other systems which were created for this particular purpose, The Simplified Spelling Society's *New Spelling* and Professor Zachrisson's *Anglic*. With the invention of Sir James Pitman's 'Augmented Roman Alphabet', or 'The Initial

Teaching Alphabet', as it has now been renamed, the situation may be said to have changed. Pitman's *i.t.a.* has been created for one purpose only—namely, to provide a kind of phonetic alphabet which will make it easier for children to learn to read ordinary English. Since the regularized spelling for English which I have proposed, may also be used for this purpose, there are now two alternative plans for dealing with the reading problem, in addition to the methods that have been used in the past and which are still used, I suppose, in well over 95 per cent of the country's schools.

The problem of teaching reading to English-speaking children is such a difficult, important and controversial question, that the greatest caution should be exercised in dealing with it. It seems to me therefore that the two new methods that have now been suggested for a solution of the problem, should be subjected to the most careful examination and comparison, before any one of them is recommended for extensive use in the schools. Such a procedure is the only one that is compatible with true scholarship. It seems to me that it is the business of the universities to study the question and to make their recommendations. It would be interesting to know, for example, whether Sir James Pitman's *i.t.a.* has as yet been approved by any department of English or linguistics at any British university. For my own part I must say that I doubt very much whether it is advisable to leave such an important matter entirely in the hands of the Local Education Authorities.

Since *i.t.a.* and Regularized Inglish are both intended to make it easier for children to learn to read, it will be of great interest to compare the different ways in which they try to achieve their common purpose. There is certainly not much resemblance between them, but in one respect they are in full agreement. In order to teach reading more rapidly and successfully it is essential according to both to employ a transitional spelling system which should be regular in character. This is of special importance to the large proportion of children who are usually classified as backward readers. Since the latter cannot be picked out from the rest of the children right from the start, it becomes more or less necessary to use the same method of teaching reading for all children.

It is indeed a sad reflection on the present English spelling system that it should be considered necessary to resort to such drastic methods in order to teach children to read. But I am inclined to think that now that the *i.t.a.* experiment has started and seems to be spreading like wildfire, to judge from the *i.t.a. Jurnal*, the English will find it increasingly difficult to go on unconcernedly with the old traditional methods. For this much is certain. Since *i.t.a.* is a kind of roughly phonetic spelling, it will be much easier for children to learn to read by its help than by the old methods. Any fairly consistent spelling is easier to learn to read than the present one. That has been proved over and over again in the past and should not need proving any more. Judging from Mr Harrison's book, *Instant Reading*, it would even seem that children who have learnt to read by *i.t.a.*, have no great difficulty in transferring to ordinary English. As far as the 70 per cent of the children are concerned who are able to learn to read the traditional spelling without too much difficulty, this is not very surprising. But the remainder, too, generally manage to transfer, though, according to Mr Harrison, it may take up to 21 months before all the children have learnt to read ordinary English. That is a very good result, even though it is not exactly what everybody would like to call 'instant reading'.

Let us then in the light of this indubitable initial success of the *i.t.a.* experiment try to imagine what the course of development is likely to be in the years to come, if it goes on in the way it has begun. Since the reading problem exists to a larger or smaller extent all over the country, it would seem to me that sooner or later practically every primary school in the country will be faced with the decision whether to use the *i.t.a.* method or not. Seeing that, with the traditional system of spelling, more than a quarter of the nation's children are doomed to remain backward readers, at least up to the age of 15, it seems highly probable that in the course of time more and more schools will be tempted to adopt the new method. Its author probably hopes that it will eventually spread to every single school in the country.

Is this then a development that the English, and the other English-speaking peoples, can view with equanimity? For my own part I do not find the prospect very cheerful. To me *i.t.a.* looks like a caricature of the English language. But perhaps I am taking too serious a view of the matter. Many people will probably think that since the new method is only a temporary thing which will be dropped as soon as children have learnt to read, it will not matter very much, if a special, strange kind of spelling and printing is used during the first or the first two schoolyears.

If the prospect for the future development that I have just sketched, should not appeal to the English-speaking peoples, the only alternative for a solution of the reading problem that we have to fall back upon, is the one provided by Regularized Inglish. It is my conviction that an experiment with this system of spelling will show that by its help children can learn to read just as rapidly and successfully as by the help of *i.t.a.*, and that in various other respects Regularized Inglish is greatly preferable to the latter.

May I in conclusion, and as a basis for further discussion, give a brief summary of the main features which characterize these two spelling systems. I have arranged them under four points for Regularized Inglish and under five for *i.t.a.* I will begin with my own system.

1. Regularized Inglish offers a reformed system of spelling for English which is sufficiently phonetic in character to permit of its being taught in accordance with definite rules of pronunciation. It employs the traditional alphabet and uses its various letters and combinations of letters in the same way as they are normally used in the present orthography. It preserves the traditional spelling in about 90 per cent of the total vocabulary, but abolishes all irregular spellings and replaces them by regular ones.

2. Regularized Inglish can be used simply as a new, more efficient method for teaching reading but keeps the way open

to a future spelling reform, in case it should prove desirable to carry out such a reform.

3. Regularized Inglish gives a clear idea of the general structure of the present English spelling system and shows what are its regular and its irregular features.

4. With its simplified spelling Regularized Inglish is eminently suitable for use as a medium of international communication. On account of its reliable and comparatively simple rules of pronunciation it can be taught with ease both to such foreigners as have already learnt to read their own native language, and to the inhabitants of developing countries who may not have any literature in their own language or who may not at present have any written language at all. In addition, the close agreement in spelling between Regularized Inglish and ordinary English makes it extremely easy to transfer from the former to the latter, in reading as well as writing. As far as mere reading is concerned, books in traditional orthography would be accessible without any difficulty.

From Regularized Inglish I will pass on to *i.t.a.*, for which a specimen has been supplied on p. 87f below.

1. *i.t.a.* also offers a system of spelling which is regular in character and therefore makes it comparatively easy to learn to read. It employs a new, strange-looking alphabet, which contains 21 additional characters and which therefore requires special type in order to print it. According to Mr Harrison's book, *Instant Reading*, (p. 117) it preserves the traditional spelling in about 50 per cent of the vocabulary. Children who have learnt to read by *i.t.a.* generally seem to be able to transfer to ordinary English after 4 to 6 terms.

2. Since *i.t.a.* employs special new symbols for the long sounds of the five simple vowels it may be somewhat easier to learn to read than Regularized Inglish, but this is far from certain and needs to be investigated. Seeing that Regularized Inglish resembles ordinary English much more closely than *i.t.a.*, it ought to be considerably easier to transfer from the former than from the latter.

3. *i.t.a.* gives no information concerning the general

structure of the present spelling system and is rather calculated to give the impression that the present system is completely irregular.

It is characteristic of ordinary English that it often employs several different symbols to render one and the same speech sound. This is particularly true of the long sounds of the simple vowels but also applies to the other long vowel sounds and to certain consonant sounds (cf. *Regularized English*, pp. 43-45).

Thus we have in ordinary English five *regular* spellings for the long *a*-sound, as found for instance in 'sale, sail, way, vein, they' (plus *eigh*, as in 'weigh'); four *regular* spellings for the long *e*-sound, as found in 'be, see, sea, piece'; five *regular* spellings for the long *i*-sound, as found in 'write, by, lie, lye, right'; three *regular* spellings for the long *o*-sound, as found in 'go, boat, toe'; five *regular* spellings for the long *u*-sound, as found in 'duty, due, neuter, new, suit'; five *regular* spellings for the long *oo*-sound, as found in 'moon, flu, blue, blew, fruit'; five *regular* spellings for the *au*-sound, as found in 'cause, saw, caught, sort, board'; three *regular* spellings for the identical sound of final or preconsonantal *er*, *ir*, *ur*, as found in 'serve, first, burn'; three *regular* spellings for the sound of *air*, as found in 'care, pair, their'; and four *regular* spellings for the sound of *eer*, as found in 'here, beer, ear, pier'.

In Regularized Inglish all the above spellings have been preserved, since they provide fully adequate guidance as to the pronunciation and since they enable us to distinguish in writing between words that are identical in sound, such for instance as the following:

mail—male, pray—prey, meet—meat, peace—piece, die—dye, side—sighed, write—right, rode—road, blue—blew, birth—berth, serf—surf, fir—fur, etc. (cf. *Regularized English*, pp. 37-38).

In *i.t.a.*, which is mainly a modification of the Simplified Spelling Society's phonetic system of spelling (cf. p. 59 above), the long sounds of the five simple vowels are consistently rendered by the ligatures æ, ee, ie, œ, ue, whatever

81

their spellings in ordinary English. The essential difference between *i.t.a.* and the Simplified Spelling Society's *New Spelling* is that the digraphs *ae*, *ee*, *ie*, *oe*, *ue* of the latter have been replaced by the ligatures just cited above, a change which I am inclined to regard as a deterioration rather than an improvement, since they seem to me indistinct and rather clumsy, un-English and difficult to write for children and since they require special type in order to print them. It should also be noted that they do not offer any better guidance as to the pronunciation than the spellings of Regularized Inglish. Since each one of the ligatures corresponds to three, four or five different spellings in ordinary English, it is quite obvious, too, that they will rather be a hindrance than a help in learning to spell ordinary English correctly.

Although on the whole it may be said that *i.t.a.*, as far as the vowel sounds of stressed syllables are concerned, adheres to the phonetic principle of 'one sign—one sound', we find that it abandons this principle in certain important respects. Thus it renders the long /ə:/-sound which occurs in final and preconsonantal positions, by the three symbols *er*, *ir*, *ur* in accordance with the usage in ordinary English, except that Pitman has introduced a special kind of *r*, '𝼀', in these combinations, in my opinion a completely useless, not to say absurd innovation.—We further find two symbols, au and *or*, for the long /ə:/-sound which occurs in such words as 'cause, saw, caught, sort, board, course'. au is employed in the first three and *or* in the last three, in close agreement with the usage in ordinary English.—Another peculiar deviation from the phonetic principle is the use in *i.t.a.* of the same symbol, the ligature æ, for the two very different sounds that occur in such words as 'name' and 'care'.—æ is further also employed in unstressed position to render a third vowel sound, the short sound /ɪ/, which occurs in the ending of such words as 'passage, manage, accurate, fountain', etc.—We may also note the use of ue for the two different sounds that are normally found in such words as for example 'cure' and 'nature'.—As far as the spellings of the vowel sounds of unstressed syllables are concerned, it may be said that on the whole *i.t.a.* abandons every claim to adherence to the phonetic principle and as a rule simply preserves the spellings that are found in ordinary English.

Passing on to the consonant sounds, we find that here, too, ordinary English spelling sometimes employs several symbols to render one and the same speech sound.

Thus we have three *regular* spellings for the *j*-sound, as found in 'jest, gem, bridge'; three *regular* spellings for the *k*-sound, as found in 'cat, king, queen, skate, scare, square' (plus *x* for /ks/, as in 'tax'); three *regular* spellings for the voiceless *s*-sound, as found in 'side, certain, case, place, scene' (plus *x* for /ks/, as in 'tax'); and five *regular* spellings for the *sh*-sound, as found in 'ship, nation, tension, mission, special'.

In Regularized Inglish the above spellings have always been preserved, since they provide fully adequate or sufficient guidance as to the pronunciation. Only exceptionally do the different spellings serve to distinguish words which are identical in sound, as for example in 'site'—'cite', 'sent'—'cent'—'scent', 'seen'—'scene'.

In *i.t.a.* the treatment of the consonant sounds presents a very peculiar compromise between the requirements of the phonetic principle and the spellings of ordinary English. In order to preserve as great a resemblance as possible to traditional orthography, *i.t.a.* frequently abandons the phonetic principle, when this can be done without causing uncertainty as regards the pronunciation.

Thus in addition to the regular spelling *j* for the *j*-sound *i.t.a.* retains the spelling *dg* in those words in which it is now used, as in 'judge, bridge'. But it replaces *g* by *j* in words such as 'gem, geography' and even *gg* by *jj* in 'exaggerate'.—*i.t.a.* further retains *c*, *k* and *ck* for the *k*-sound in such words as 'cat, king, duck' (and even in *cemist* for 'chemist'), but it replaces *q* and *x* by *k* and *ks* in words such as *kween*, *taks* (and further *x* by *gz* in words such as 'exact, exist').—For the voiceless *s*-sound *i.t.a.* always writes *s*. It thus replaces *c* and *sc* by *s* in words such as 'certain, cell, place, accent, scene', although the rules for the distribution of the *s*- and *k*-sounds for *c* and *sc* in ordinary English are exceedingly simple and reliable. The *s*-sound is used before *e*, *i* and *y* and the *k*-sound in all other positions. We only find one or two exceptions in the whole language.—For the *sh*-sound *i.t.a.* introduces a new letter, the ligature ʃh, a combination of the regular phonetic symbol for the *sh*-sound and *h*. It is difficult to see why this new character should be any easier for children to read than the regular digraph *sh*. Even in cases like næʃhon, speʃhial, penʃhon, paʃhon one must ask whether it is really worth while introducing this new spelling with ʃh and whether it is not just as simple to give the rule that the combinations 'ti, ci, si, ssi' before an unstressed syllable are to be pronounced as *sh*, especially in view of the fact that children would have to learn these spellings anyway, when after about a year or a year and a half they would have to transfer to ordinary English spelling.— A further instance of *i.t.a.*'s abandonment of the phonetic principle is afforded by its treatment of the double consonants that are found in traditional orthography. They have always been retained in *i.t.a.*, although in a phonetic system of spelling there is no reason for employing double consonant letters.

Besides the symbol ʃh for the *sh*-sound *i.t.a.* introduces five more ligatures for consonant sounds, ᴄh, ʈh, ᴅh, wh, ŋ, which are found in such words as 'child, thin, this, why, sing'. In addition to these we find in *i.t.a.* eight more ligatures for vowel sounds, the five already mentioned above for the long sounds of the simple vowels and further the three that are used to represent the vowel sounds found in such words as 'cause, saw, noise, boy, out, now', namely au, oi and ou. The reason for joining the letters together, which makes it impossible to print them with ordinary type, appears to be that the author of *i.t.a.* wishes to turn them into alphabetical units, because he considers digraphs to be too difficult for children to learn. But such is certainly not the case, and if it did sometimes prove desirable to show that two letters belong together, this could just as easily be done by the simple expedient of underlining them. It is not the digraphs as such that are difficult; it is the fact that they so often represent a number of totally different sounds in the existing orthography. This is particularly true with regard to the vowel digraphs but also applies to some of the digraphs which represent consonant sounds.

After the above survey of the important differences between *i.t.a.* and Regularized Inglish I will now try to sum up briefly what I consider to be the most characteristic features of these two spelling systems.

From our analysis it appears that *i.t.a.* presents *an essentially new system of spelling for English*, which, though highly inconsistent, is considerably more "phonetic" in character than that of Regularized Inglish. It is, however, an artificial system which has very little to do with ordinary English spelling. Owing in particular to the great differences between *i.t.a.* and traditional orthography with regard to the representation of the various long vowel sounds, it is obvious that the transfer from *i.t.a.* to ordinary English is bound to cause very great difficulties. When we find that it is possible to teach children to read more easily by the aid of *i.t.a.* than by the usual present method, i.e. through a combination of the 'whole word method' and phonics, this only goes to prove that any reasonably 'phonetic' or regular spelling is better than the dreadful jumble of regular and irregular spellings that we now find in ordinary English.

The essential characteristic feature of Regularized Inglish is that *it is **not** a new system of spelling for English*. It is in fact nothing but the regular system of spelling that is inherent in ordinary English and which emerges when we eliminate the 5 to 10 per cent of irregular spellings in the language and replace them by regular ones. Though this system is considerably more complicated than a pure phonetic system of spelling, the important thing is that it is *regular* and therefore can be taught according to definite rules of pronunciation, such as we find in other languages with reasonably "phonetic" spelling systems. A summary of these rules will be found in Chapter IX of my book, *Regularized English*, pp. 303–312. It goes without saying that the transfer to ordinary English spelling will hardly cause any difficulties. Cf. specimen on p. 88 below.

4. Since *i.t.a.* provides a kind of roughly phonetic spelling which resembles ordinary English, it is only to be expected that it will make it comparatively easier for native speakers to learn to read. For foreigners, on the other hand, who have already learnt to read their own language, reading English, as distinct from pronouncing it, does not in itself present any problem. If they belong to nations using the Roman alphabet, they will be able to read most English words at first sight, though of course without the proper pronunciation and without understanding them. For these foreigners it is the pronunciation of the words that they come across in written English that constitutes the major difficulty, besides the acquisition of a sufficient vocabulary. In order to cope with this difficulty they have usually found it necessary to employ a special phonetic transcription, for example the one recommended by the International Phonetic Association, which we find in most modern textbooks and dictionaries. It goes without saying that the adoption of such a reform of English spelling as we find in Regularized Inglish, would enormously facilitate the learning of the language for all foreign students, since it would eliminate the vast majority of irregular spellings and thus as a rule make it possible to infer the pronunciation from the spelling.

For the inhabitants of developing countries, who only speak their own native language and who may or may not have learnt to read it, or read it in a non-Roman script, *i.t.a.* will undoubtedly be far easier to learn to read than ordinary English; but since (unlike native English speakers) they have not learnt to speak English, the transition from *i.t.a.* to ordinary English spelling is bound to cause very great difficulties—far greater than for native speakers of English. It would obviously be far easier for them to transfer to ordinary English, if they had first learnt to read the language in the form of Regularized Inglish.

5. *i.t.a.* offers no new system of spelling for English that could be used eventually to *replace* the present one. On the

contrary one might even say that by instituting something that can *only* be a transition to traditional spelling, it virtually blocks the way to any future reform. Since a reform of English spelling is essential, if we want to make English an auxiliary language for the whole world, the general adoption of *i.t.a.* for teaching reading in the English-speaking countries would put a very effective obstacle in the way of such a development.

There are a good many things I would have liked to add on the structure of *i.t.a.* as a phonetic alphabet[1], but I am afraid I may already have taxed your patience to the utmost; so I think I had better stop here. If I were to sum up my views on *i.t.a.* in just one sentence, I would say that for the purpose of teaching children to read, the *i.t.a.* script is a wholly unnecessary invention. Such advantages as may be claimed for it can be obtained equally well by means of the regular alphabet, if the English-speaking peoples were willing to use a transitional spelling system for the first two schoolyears. By substituting regular spellings for the irregular ones, they can gain the more immediate end, which is to make it easier for English-speaking children to learn to read and write, and at the same time ensure the ulterior purpose of making their language a fitter instrument for national as well as international communication.

From M. Harrison, *Instant Reading*, p. 104.

### a spesimen ov i.t.a. printiŋ

ie hav just cum from a scœl whær ꝼhe nue reediŋ iz taut. ie met ꝼhær a littl girl ov siks. ʃhee iꭍ ꝼhe œldest ov a larj family liviŋ on an œldham housiŋ estæt. tœ yeerꭍ agœ ʃhee woꭍ a ʃhie nervus ꝑhield, tœ frietend tœ tauk. ʃhee haꭍ wun priezd personal poꭍꭍeʃhon—a dog-eerd anꝑholojy ov verꭍ, given tœ her bie an œlder ꝑhield. ꝼhat littl girl ov siks haꭍ just red tœ mee very buetifœlly wurꭍwurꝼh's daffodilꭍ. ie askt her whie ʃhee ꝑhœꭍ ꝼhat pœem. ʃhee replied ꝼhat ʃhee luvd daffodilꭍ.

1. This aspect of *i.t.a.* has been dealt with by the author in his article, "i.t.a. versus Regularized English", published in the April–May number 1968 of the American journal *Education*, pp. 300–307.

tœdæ ʃhee speeks wiʈh ʧarm and confidens. ʈhe œnly critisiʓm ov heɾ reediŋ ov ʈhe pœem miet bee ʈhat ʃhee red it raʈheɾ kwickly, tœ neerly at ʈhe speed ov sielent reediŋ. ʃhee found ʈhe pæj in ʈhe bœk bie lœkiŋ up ʈhe pœet's næm in ʈhe alfabetical indeks.

œnly ʈhe siɾcumstanseʓ ov ʈhat story ɑr novel. ʈhe aʧheevment ov ʈhat littl girl ov siks yeerʓ iʓ ov itself færly commonplæs in œldham nouadæʓ.

octœber, 1963

*A Specimen ov i.t.a. printing* (rewritten in Regularized Inglish)

I hav just cum from a scoole whare the new reading iz taught. I met thare a little girl ov six. She iz the oldest ov a large family living on an Oldham houzing estate. Too years ago she woz a shy nervous childe, too frightend to tauk. She haz wun prized personal pozession—a dog-eard anthology ov verse, given to her by an older childe. That little girl ov six haz just red to me very beutifully Wordsworth's *Daffodils*. I aaskt her why she choze that poem. She replied that she luvd daffodils.

Today she speaks widh charm and confidence. The oenly criticizm ov her reading ov the poem might be that she red it raadher quickly, too nearly at the speed ov silent reading. She found the page in the book by looking up the poet's name in the alfabetical index.

Oenly the circumstances ov that story ar novel. The achievment ov that little girl ov six years iz ov itself fairly commonplace in Oldham nowadays.

October, 1963

# 4

# New Spelling with Old Letters

*by*

## P. A. D. MacCarthy

A NUMBER of inescapable choices face the would-be reformer of English spelling, and it will be well at the outset to outline what these are: the initial choice is between retaining the roman alphabet (the traditional 26-letter orthography of present-day English) and discarding it in favour of some other alphabet.

A decision in principle to retain it forces upon one the awkward problem of what to do about the major inadequacy of the roman alphabet when working out a satisfactory orthography for English, namely the fact that it contains too few letters to go round, in view of the more numerous sounds of the English language (any form of the English language) than the 26 letters available—assuming of course that one is proposing to apply the first principle of true alphabetic writing, that is, one written symbol for each sound.

It follows that it is essential to extend the possibilities of the traditional roman letters by one means or another, and here a number of alternatives present themselves, each with its attendant advantages and (more often) disadvantages. One possibility is to introduce into the system (or rather, to accept within it, since it is already there) the concept of the *digraph*, that is, two successive letters for the regular representation of single sounds. English is already quite familiar with this type of extension of romanic script, e.g., *sh*, *th* for single consonant sounds, *ee*, *ea*, etc. for simple vowels. Most languages employing the basic forms of the roman alphabet make a greater or lesser use of digraphic spellings, but the trouble with most of them—and this applies to English—is that they do not make *sufficient* use of them for all needs and/or they do not make *consistent* use of them. Moreover, a digraph may itself be ambiguous, as when the spellings *sh*, *th* do not have to be interpreted digraphically in *mishap*, *foothold*, and again when *read* may rhyme with *reed* or with *red*. By consistent use I mean the unvarying representation of a given sound by a given pair of letters: that this is not the case in present English spelling is readily exemplified in words such as *bishop*, *mission*, *nation*, *ocean* and the like, or conversely in *bough*, *cough*, *though*, *tough*, *through*, etc. (It is irrelevant to the present argument that different languages make inconsistent use of a given digraph as between one another—though this may be held to be regrettable, and is undoubtedly initially confusing to the learner of foreign languages. Thus both Polish and Hungarian use the digraph *sz*, but Polish orthography consistently uses it for English sh-sound, Hungarian uses it consistently for English s-sound.)

If English spelling were to utilise the digraph to the extent needed for supplementing the roman letters used singly, many more digraphs than at present would be required. It is often not fully realized by the ordinary person *how* inadequate the roman alphabet is from this point of view (there is no need at this point to outline some of its other inadequacies), and therefore how considerable the changes would have to be before a really satisfactory, consistent, unambiguous and exception-free spelling system, using roman letters, resulted. The elimination of all unpronounced letters (*psalm*, *right*), including repeated consonants (*letter*, *ball*) would be merely a beginning—and would of course create its own problems of alternative representation. Digraphs, if accepted as the sole solution, would have to be used much more extensively, especially for writing vowels—since it is here that the roman alphabet is proportionately more deficient: of the 26 letters, only five are in regular use for vowels (*y* being used irregularly), whereas the English language possesses about 20 vowel distinctions—as compared with some 24 consonants, which is not a great many fewer than the roman letters available to represent them uniliterally.

The major objection to digraphs, as such, arises as soon as the aims of economy are taken into account. One of the most powerful arguments in favour of spelling reform in general is that of *savings* of various kinds—saving of children's learning time, of the writer's writing time, of typists' and printers' wages, of paper, ink, transport, storage, and so on—to the extent to which these might be achieved. Now the use of digraphs must conflict with any savings obtained by the elimination of unnecessary letters (about one letter in six is superfluous at present), and the more extensive their use, the more are those savings nullified. Other things being equal, it must be the case that two letters take twice as long to write as one, and use twice as much paper and ink.

A very widely used alternative to digraphs is that of *accents*—marks placed above or below an existing letter to give it a different value from that to be inferred when the mark is absent. English happens to be almost entirely free from accentual marks, but French orthography has several (not by any means efficiently used for discriminating between sounds, however, since an accent on the letter *a*, e.g., *à* or *â*, does not consistently alter its sound; and *è* and *ê* invariably sound alike), while Polish and especially Hungarian have a very large number. Consistently used, as they are for these last two languages, accents undoubtedly provide an effective means for increasing the number of written distinctions. Their main disadvantages are calligraphic and typographical: any handwritten stroke that has to be added separately, that does not form part of a letter, is a nuisance and either wastes time or tends to get left out—even the dotting of *i*'s and the crossing of *t*'s, so traditional that they are not looked upon as 'accents', are troublesome here; printers find accents, being

91

so small, are easily broken, and through wear soon give an indistinct impression on paper; the number of type sorts required to cope with many accented letters is a problem for the printer, as it is for the typewriter keyboard; so is the accenting of capital letters.

A proliferation of accents on the printed page produces an impression of dazzle trying to the eyes, and a tendency to blur the characteristic outline of the printed word seen as a black shape on the white surface, making individual words less readily recognizable—an important consideration when rapid and effortless reading is the aim.

Retention of the roman alphabet, as such, does not preclude its extension by additional letters; yet this device, in the long history of romanic script, has met with little success. The great difficulty has been to devise fresh letter shapes that shall be good enough to harmonize with the existing ones —in upper and lower case, and in all founts of type, as well as in handwriting—yet at the same time distinctive enough to be recognizably different, even in unfavourable conditions of size, visibility, etc. They should also remain sufficiently simple in their basic shape not to add much to the number of pen movements required to form them by hand, nor to their lateral extension on the paper, as compared with the existing letters themselves. It is noteworthy that only *i* and *j*; *u*, *v* and *w* have differentiated themselves into distinct letters *within* the roman alphabet in the course of many centuries, whereas only a very few other additions, e.g., Danish ø, Icelandic *æ* and ð, have proved acceptable for the limited purpose of a single language. Contrast with this paucity of successful invention of new letter shapes the very extensive use of accents applied to, but forming no organic part of, known letters—with the results outlined in the preceding paragraphs.

Here again, the scale on which invention of additional letters would be demanded is the main obstacle to its success: if two or three letters only had been required for English, they would doubtless have been evolved long since; but to produce nearly a score of new shapes such as would commend themselves to expert and public alike, sufficiently powerfully to secure wide approval and eventual official adoption—this has so far defeated all those calligraphers and type designers, whether amateur or professional, who have from time to time made the attempt. It is ironic that the wide variations as between majuscule and minuscule, printed and cursive shapes, that have grown up over the centuries *within* the roman tradition, should not themselves be available as satisfactory letters to exist alongside one another and augment the basic alphabet—the reasons being mainly twofold: first, the confusion that would be created in the minds of existing users, and thus the instinctive rejection by those users of any proposal to employ, say, the shape B with a value consistently different from b, and so forth (just as they also tend to reject the idea of the redeployment of the—for English—redundant letters *c*, *q* and *x* for, e.g., the English sounds ch, ng and sh, respectively); secondly, the actual design of many of the existing alternative shapes (A, a, ɑ, etc.) would not lend each of them equally well to separate, all-purpose use; for instance, many of our present capitals would be unsatisfactory as cursive forms, many lower-case forms typographically objectionable as capitals, and so on.

Theoretically it is of course not essential that either digraphs or accents should be used exclusively: some combination of the two devices might be preferable, and this is indeed what is done in a great many romanic orthographies—Polish, for instance, employs a certain number of digraphs and a certain number of accented letters. In practice, however, this must be looked upon as at best a compromise solution, embodying in a certain measure the weaknesses inherent in the use of digraphs and of accents as such, and without the logical, systematic or aesthetic unity that should be looked for.

The system of spelling that I wish to outline to you today has evolved over some sixty years and, known now as New Spelling (or Nue Speling), it is the scheme approved and sponsored by the Simplified Spelling Society of Great Britain. I should point out that neither I personally, nor the individual members of the Society who have been the prime movers in establishing New Spelling in all its details, are necessarily of the opinion that this particular system of spelling reform is the best possible and worthy of adoption in preference to all other systems, whether extant or potential. What is fairly clear, in my view, is that, given the set of principles underlying the scheme (and I will detail these in a moment, together with the main reasons for their adoption), the choice and arrangement of letters is indeed the best possible, and no material improvement along these lines is obtainable, in view of the very thorough investigation of our present spelling, and the painstaking assessment of alternatives at each point, that have preceded the setting up of the proposed orthography in question.

The guiding principles on which New Spelling has been based are as follows:

(1) *No new characters to be introduced.*

(2) *No new accents or diacritics to be introduced, and detached marks as such to be used in any case as sparingly as possible.*

Thus the Society's self-imposed terms of reference confine its activity to demonstrating what can be done with the existing roman letters, minus any found to be unnecessary. It follows that the digraphic representation of single sounds (already traditional in English spelling, as has been shown above) has to be extended quite considerably, thus giving priority to other considerations than those of economy of materials and, to some extent, time. But the choice of letters for digraphs is to be governed by the further principle:

(3) *Unused or relatively unfamiliar combinations of letters to be avoided as far as possible* (though some exceptions to this are inevitable).

(4) *Current usage to remain unaltered wherever common sense and expediency suggest.* This 'principle of least disturbance' means that as far as possible each sound should be written with its most habitual single letter (or pair of letters).

This leads to a large number of straightforward decisions, some others that can be reached only on the basis of statistical counts and a careful weighing of pros and cons, and a residue of instances where, even after this has been done, the case is so nicely balanced that an arbitrary choice has ultimately to be made.

(5) *Each symbol (letter or digraph) to be self-contained, that is, its significance not to depend on any other letter in the sequence.* This precludes, e.g., the doubling of consonant letters to indicate the (short) value of the preceding vowel.

(6) *The complete scheme to be thorough-going, simple, regular and free from exceptions and anomalies, economical, easy to learn and to use, and no concessions to be made to the habits of a generation brought up on our present spelling, if future generations might thereby be inconvenienced.* This last point obviously conflicts with the principle of least disturbance which, if pursued to its logical conclusion, would clearly lead to no change at all; thus the final principle is in this case the overriding one.

Two main reasons can be given for the Society's advocacy of the line of action embodied in the foregoing recommendations: the advantages of continuity with past tradition, thus making a transition relatively easy for the living generation and the reading of older texts still possible for later generations without much special study; and the practical issue of securing essential public favour at the outset, without arousing more than the inevitable amount of disapproval and out-of-hand rejection on the grounds of novelty and strangeness.

At this point it will be well to provide a specimen text printed in New Spelling, so that you may without more delay see for yourself just what New Spelling looks like, and begin to appreciate the kind of thing that is involved when an orthography for English is worked out in accordance with the above principles. Here it is:

Forskor and seven yeerz agoe our faadherz braut forth on dhis kontinent a nue naeshon, konseevd in liberti, and dedikaeted to dhe propozishon dhat aul men ar kreeaeted eekwal.

Nou we ar en.gaejd in a graet sivil wor, testing whedher dhat naeshon, or eni naeshon soe konseevd and soe dedikaeted, kan long enduer. We ar met on a graet batlfeeld ov dhat wor. We hav kum to dedikaet a porshon ov dhat feeld az a fienal resting-plaes for dhoez huu gaev dhaer lievz dhat dhat naeshon miet liv. It iz aultogedher fiting and proper dhat we shood duu dhis.

But in a larjer sens, we kanot dedikaet—we kanot konsekraet—we kanot haloe—dhis ground. Dhe braev men, living and ded, huu strugld heer, hav konsekraeted it far abuv our puur pou.er to ad or detrakt. Dhe wurld wil litl noet nor long remember whot we sae heer, but it kan never forget whot dhae did heer. It iz for us, dhe living, raadher, to be dedikaeted heer to dhe unfinisht wurk which dhae huu faut heer hav dhus far soe noebli advaanst. It iz raadher for us to be heer dedikaeted to dhe graet taask remaening befor us—dhat from dheez onord ded we taek inkreest devoeshon to dhat kauz for which dhae gaev dhe laast fool mezher ov devoeshon; dhat we heer hieli rezolv dhat dheez ded shal not hav died in vaen; dhat dhis naeshon, under God, shal hav a nue burth ov freedom; and dhat guvernment ov dhe peepl, bie dhe peepl, for dhe peepl, shal not perish from dhe urth.

Now before I go into any detailed exposition of the system, let me make two general points, which will no doubt have occurred to many of you while reading the foregoing specimen. The first point worth making is surely this: that although you may have been held up in your reading momentarily by this word or that, and although (if you have never looked at New Spelling before) you must have been struck initially by the appearance of many words, nevertheless you *were* able to make out the passage—in other words, New Spelling can be read at sight. In fact about a third of all words, including an even higher proportion of the commonest words, are spelt in New Spelling as they are spelt now; a further third at least are only very slightly changed, and still others, though more extensively altered, are none the less immediately recognizable. Of course if you were already to know the relevant facts as to which letters stand for which sounds in the system, you should have no difficulty in reading *all* words at sight.

Secondly, usage as regards spacing, punctuation and capitalization remains unaltered. It would be perfectly possible to use New Spelling and, for instance, abolish all capitals, or write question-marks at the beginning as well as at the end of each question-sentence, as is done in Spanish, but these things are not themselves part and parcel of New Spelling.

It should next be pointed out that the text of the above passage (it is of course Abraham Lincoln's famous Gettysburg Address) is rendered into an *English* pronunciation, though obviously originally spoken with an American one. This enables me to draw attention to the fact that New Spelling allows for a certain amount of regional variation in pronunciation to be shown, as regards the distribution of sounds (thus an American would probably say, and could therefore write, *advanst* where most forms of British English would have *advaanst*), but that a general-purpose orthography is most effective when designed to show the essential linguistic distinctions only, and not all the other personal or regional differences; and in fact a true New Spelling version of an American rendering of the passage need differ from the above in no more than perhaps half a dozen places. The almost complete standardization of spellings which the New Spelling system makes possible is naturally of great practical importance where the printing of books for world-wide use is involved, but at the same time a fair number of existing alternative pronunciations of individual words (alternatives even for British speakers) can in fact be indicated, and would then be likely to appear in, for instance, personal correspondence. A complete dictionary of New Spelling would therefore list the alternative spellings possible within the framework of the system.

It is sometimes said that New Spelling is easy to master

because the basic facts of the system can be stated 'on a postcard'. Whether this is literally true or not, I propose to set out first the sound-symbol relationships in New Spelling schematically, and then to make a few additional observations.

The representation of the consonants can be rapidly grasped after an examination of the following table of New Spellings, when checked against the present spellings in the table beneath. The letters representing the sounds illustrated are printed *in capitals*.

New Spelling

| Pin | Tin | Kin | | |
|-----|-----|-----|-----|-----|
| Bin | Din | Got | | |
| Fat | THing | Set | SHut | Hot |
| Vat | DHis | Zest | viZHon | (loKH) |
| Met | Net | siNG | | |
| | | (thiNk, fiNGger) | | |
| CHat | | | WHim | |
| Jet | Let | Rot | Win | Yet |

Present Spelling

| pin | tin | kin | | |
|-----|-----|-----|-----|-----|
| bin | din | got | | |
| fat | thing | set | shut | hot |
| vat | this | zest | vision | (loch) |
| met | net | sing | | |
| | | (think, finger) | | |
| chat | | | whim | |
| jet | let | rot | win | yet |

Now here are the vowels shown in the same way.

New Spelling

| hAt | pEt | hIt | hOt | hUt | fOOt |
|------|------|------|------|------|------|
| fAEt | fEEt | fIEt | gOEt | fUEd | mUUn |
| fAER | fEER | fIER | lOER | pUER | pUUR |

98

| kAAm | kOIn | kAUl | | kOUnt |
| fARm | | shORt | tURn | sOUR |
| stARi | | stORi | fURi | |
| | | | | |
| kARRi | | sORRi | hURRi | sistER |

## Present Spelling

| hat | pet | hit | hot | hut | foot |
| fate | { feet | fight | goat | feud | moon |
| | { feat | | | | |
| { fare | fear | fire | lower | pure | poor |
| { fair | | | | | |
| | | | | | |
| calm | coin | call | | | count |
| farm | | short | turn | | sour |
| starry | | story | furry | | |
| carry | | sorry | hurry | | sister |

*Note* 1. The letters Q and X are not used, being redundant, as the examples below will show, and C only appears in CH, for the same reason. (In the interests of economy, the sound written with CH could well be written just with C, but the desire not to break too much with tradition suggested that the retention of CH was expedient, at any rate to begin with, since spellings such as *curc* for church, *woc* for watch, might be too novel to prove readily acceptable.)

| Present spelling | Example | N.S. | Example |
| --- | --- | --- | --- |
| C | cat | k | kat |
| | cell | s | sel |
| | accept | ks | aksept |
| | ocean | sh | oeshan |
| Qu | quite | kw | kwiet |
| X | extend | ks | ekstend |
| | except | k | eksept |
| | exist | gz | egzist |
| | anxiety | z | angzie. eti |
| | anxious | (k)sh | ankshus or angshus |

99

*Note* 2. In the interests of economy, and especially so as to cause less disturbance, ten 'word-signs' for some of the most frequently recurring words in the language are in New Spelling. They are to be looked upon as 'reduced' forms, the full New Spelling that they would have (but which is never used) being shown beneath the dotted line in the table.

### New Spelling

| me | he | she | we | be | dhe |
|----|-----|------|-----|-----|------|
| I | U | a | to | wer | |

........................................................................

| mee | hee | shee | wee | bee | dhee |
|------|------|-------|------|------|-------|
| Ie | Ue | ae | too | { wur | |
| | | | (tuu) | { waer | |

### Present Spelling

| me | he | she | we | be | the |
|----|------|------|-----|------|-----|
| I | you | a | to | were | |

*Note* 3. One of the most striking departures from present usage is in the use of *dh* for the voiced sound of TH. It is particularly striking at the beginning of a word, and it so happens that about a dozen extremely common English words begin with this sound. Although the spellings *th | dh* are analogically on a par with *t | d* (as *sh | zh* are with *s | z*), and although *dh* is at least as easily formed by hand as *th*, it has been pointed out that a concession to present usage with respect to this sound, at least at the beginnings of words, would enable half of these words to remain unchanged (italicized in the table below) and the other half to resemble their present shape much more closely.

### Present Spelling

| the | this | that | these | those | though | thus |
|------|-------|-------|--------|--------|---------|-------|
| they | them | their | there | then | than | thence |

## New Spelling

| dhe | dhis | dhat | dheez | dhoez | dhoe | dhus |
|-----|------|------|-------|-------|------|------|
| dhae | dhem | dhaer | dhaer | dhen | dhan | dhens |

## Alternative New Spelling

| *the* | *this* | *that* | theez | thoez | thoe | *thus* |
|-------|--------|--------|-------|-------|------|--------|
| thae | *them* | thaer | thaer | *then* | *than* | thens |

It is doubtful whether a concession such as this (already rejected in principle, it will be recalled) would bring such advantages as to outweigh the manifest disadvantage of having this inconsistency introduced into the system, necessitating arbitrary memorization, when either the voiced th-sound would be represented initially by letters different from those used in other positions (e.g. *brudher*, *breedh*), or—supposing no *dh* spelling were admitted—the voiced th-sound would be regularly written with the same letters as the voiceless th-sound, and thus an important distinction between essential sounds of the language not shown in spelling.

Moreover, it is not easy to stop, once concessions in the interest of present spellings are admitted. For instance, it could well be argued that a number of other words (besides the ten word-signs already adopted) might be treated as word signs and simply taken over into New Spelling unchanged, with no attempt to assimilate them to the system.

It is instructive to examine the 70 commonest words in the English language.

Aside from the ten word-signs already shown, 19 words are unchanged in any case in New Spelling (as established by the word-counts used for Godfrey Dewey's *Relativ Frequency of English Speech Sounds*: and, in, it, for, on, not, at, but, or, which, from, our, an, been, him, if, when, up, out.

The 14 words having initial TH have already been listed. The remaining 27 words would be

was, as, have, by, are, his, all, will, has, one, my, so, your, can, would, what, who, do, her, time, war, any, more, now, other, say, only.

101

It is doubtful indeed whether so many exceptional and anomalous spellings should be tolerated within a system expressly designed to eliminate this kind of thing, but there is no doubt that the printed page would appear much less changed, and a high percentage of recurring words would be only slightly altered, if at all.

The present movement within the Society and its sister Simpler Spelling Association in America is rather the other way—in the direction of greater consistency, logic, and uniformity. Indeed, as recently as 1955 the two bodies met and ironed out a small number of outstanding divergences between them (by each side conceding some of the other's preferences), so that the system they now put forward is identical in all respects on both sides of the Atlantic (see p. 103).

Still other points of detail have been borne in upon me recently (which I will not go into now), where I consider still greater logicality and simplicity might be obtained in certain minor respects, but in this connection one must remember two things: first, spelling reformers have in the past often laid themselves open to criticism on the grounds that they could not agree among themselves and could not settle on a pre-ferred system, so the Society is anxious not to open the way yet again for all and sundry to come forward with their own favourite suggested modifications; and secondly, the Society itself now has a vested interest, in the shape of material already published, to call a halt to further change in the scheme they put forward. However, most of the Society's publications were in print before the 1955 modifications, and would strictly require reprinting in any case, as finance permits. Until that happens, the 1955 modifications can easily be memorized and their effects allowed for by the reader of the Society's literature.

One other point concerns the interesting innovation of a dot placed on the line within a word at the point of syllabic division wherever ambiguity in the notation might otherwise result (two instances of this occurred in the above specimen passage). This was decided upon at the 1955 meeting in

preference to either the hyphen (between juxtaposed consonants, as in *mis-hap*) or the diaeresis that had previously been
employed (in the case of juxtaposed vowels, as in *hapiëst*).
The diaeresis is now entirely eliminated, and the hyphen
reverts to its normal uses: in genuine compounds, and for
uncompleted words at the end of a line. It will be realized
that the device of the dot does constitute a diacritical mark,
and moreover an unfamiliar one in its function here, but it
would occur but rarely in any case—no more than once or
twice on a page—and in practice it would not in most cases
really need to be written or printed since ambiguity would
hardly in fact be caused if it were omitted.[1]

In conclusion let me draw attention to the important fact
that New Spelling as it stands is not adequate to deal with two
major features of English from the point of view of the foreign
learner, being designed primarily for native users, i.e. those
who already know the language. These two features are: the
incidence of strong stresses, and the pronunciation of the
vowels in weakly stressed syllables; neither of these are indicated in New Spelling. To deal with the second point first,
there is no vowel letter in the roman alphabet that could
regularly and uniquely stand for the neutral, central or schwa
vowel that occurs in such a high proportion of weakly stressed
syllables in English. The compilers of New Spelling gave
much thought to this difficult problem and decided that vowels
in unstressed syllables should in general be represented
by the letters now used in those syllables (thus *sister*, *begar*,
*aktor*, etc.). This means that the proper New Spelling of the
vowels in such syllables cannot be deduced from pronunciation, and a certain amount of arbitrary memorization of
spellings is inevitable. A minor compensatory advantage is
that the relation between a number of cognate words is still
able to be shown (thus *foetograaf*, *fotografer*, *foetografik*), in

1. Author's Note: More recently still (1967), the American body has
shown signs of wishing to make a number of concessions to present
usage, but the British have been unable to agree to incorporating these in
the official New Spelling, on the grounds that they would detract from
the consistency and rigour of the system.

cases where the shift of stress is in speech accompanied by altered vowel qualities. The only alternative would be to spell the unstressed central vowel always with a special, additional letter, and this is of course not available within the existing alphabet and is thus excluded from the possibilities open to New Spelling.

As regards stressing, once the place of strong stress in a word is known (as it is known to speakers of their own language), most of the proper New Spellings of words are automatically determined and words so spelt can be read off without difficulty. For those uncertain of the place of strong stress, reading and correct spelling may sometimes present more of a problem. But there would be no theoretical objection to a mark of stress (e.g. an acute accent) placed on the appropriate syllable (thus *fóetograaf*, *fotógrafer*, *foetográfik*), as an indication to the young or the non-native learner, or on unusual words for the benefit of all—except, of course, that this would constitute a further diacritical mark, of very frequent occurrence, and that it would convey superfluous information for those who already know the words.

# The Shaw Alphabet for Writers

Double lines ⁼ between pairs show the relative height of Talls, Deeps, and Shorts. Wherever possible, finish letters rightwards; those starred ★ will be written upwards. Also see heading and footnotes overleaf.

| | Tall | Deep | | | Short | Short | |
|---|---|---|---|---|---|---|---|
| **p**eep | ⟩ ⁼ ⟨ | **b**ib | | **i**f | ∣ ⁼ կ | **ea**t |
| **t**ot | ↑ ⁼ ↓ | **d**ead | | **e**gg | ∪ ⁼ ⊂ | **a**ge |
| **k**ick | ↻ ⁼ ⟗ | **g**ag | | **a**sh★ | ⟍ ⁼ ⊐ | **i**ce |
| **f**ee | ⟋ ⁼ ⟨ | **v**ow | | **a**do★ | ⟋ ⁼ 7 | **u**p |
| **th**igh | ∂ ⁼ ϱ | **th**ey | | **o**n | ⟍ ⁼ ○ | **oa**k |
| **s**o | ⟨ ⁼ ⟩ | **z**oo | | w**oo**l | V ⁼ ∧ | **oo**ze |
| **s**ure | ⟨ ⁼ ⟩ | mea**s**ure | | **ou**t | ⟨ ⁼ ⟩ | **oi**l |
| **ch**urch | ⟨ ⁼ ⟩ | **j**udge | | **ah**★ | ϛ ⁼ ⟨ | **aw**e |
| **y**ea | ⟍ ⁼ ⟋ | ★**w**oe | | **a**re | ⟲ ⁼ ⟳ | **or** |
| h**u**ng | ℓ ⁼ ɣ | **h**a-ha | | **air** | ⟑ ⁼ ⟄ | **err** |
| | Short | Short | | arr**ay** | ⟑ ⁼ ⟑ | **ear** |
| **l**oll | ⊂ ⁼ ⊃ | **r**oar | | | | Tall |
| **m**ime★ | ⟋ ⁼ ⟍ | **n**un | | **I**an | ⟧ ⁼ Ⲗ | **y**ew |

# From Lincoln's speech at Gettysburg

[Shavian alphabet text representing Lincoln's Gettysburg Address]

# 5

# The Bernard Shaw Alphabet

*by*
## P. A. D. MacCarthy

THE Bernard Shaw Alphabet (or Shavian, as it has come to be called), represents an attempt to alter the mode of writing English—and ultimately perhaps any language—that is almost diametrically opposed to all the proposals for spelling reform (in its widest sense) that have been discussed up till the present in this series,—in particular the complete opposite of the system called New Spelling that I myself spoke about here not so long ago.

New Spelling—let me remind you—involved (1) *retaining the traditional roman alphabet intact* (apart from the elimination or non-use of a couple of redundant letters); (2) *the rearrangement of the roman letters to the best advantage*—fairly ruthlessly from the standpoint of the present-day user, yet disturbing current spellings as little as possible consistent with a thoroughgoing, systematic reform—; and (3) *the liberal use of combinations of two letters to stand for single sounds*, this being a necessary evil resulting from the deficiency in number of roman letters for writing any language having more than 26 distinctive sounds.

Both the other previous speakers in this series also put forward schemes based upon the roman alphabet:—Dr. Wijk's proposals ('Regularized English') involved even less departure from traditional usage than does New Spelling—

they would leave the great bulk of current spellings intact. Sir James Pitman's Initial Teaching Alphabet, conceived as a method for speeding the process of learning to read, makes concessions to present spelling with the express aim of facilitating the transition back to it (once the reading skill as such has been acquired). Pitman's *i.t.a.* is, apart from that, based evidently on New Spelling, but, in addition, employs a number of newly-designed ligatured forms, resulting in most cases in strictly non-roman shapes (thus avoiding the New Spelling device of juxtaposing two familiar letters to form digraphs).

Now Shavian is different in kind from all of the foregoing: Shavian is a *new* alphabet. No one could read Shavian at sight simply for having learnt to read roman. Before one can read Shavian the value of each of the completely new symbols has to be learnt, and before reading from Shavian fluently the skill of scanning and interpreting the sequences of those symbols, and of recognizing the shapes of whole words from previous familiarity with those shapes, has to be acquired over a period of time. Shavian therefore represents a radical departure from tradition (though there have of course been other proposed radical departures in the past), and I should like first to deal with the motivation in the mind of its inspirer, George Bernard Shaw, so that we may more clearly understand what he was trying to bring about, and why.

As a professional writer, Shaw was struck by the wastage involved in English spelling: the waste of time spent writing by hand many silent or redundant letters (Shaw himself always wrote in Pitman's Shorthand); the waste of materials (paper, ink, etc.) used in writing those letters; the waste of time spent by every child learning to spell English words with their inconsistencies and irregularities, time spent by every teacher of children, and by every foreign learner, and teacher, of English anywhere in the world. He campaigned frequently and vigorously during his lifetime to draw people's attention to the significance of this state of affairs, and to break down their apathetic conservatism, if not their championing adherence to what he termed 'Johnsonese', for he ascribed (no doubt correctly) the standardization of our present spelling largely to the publication and subsequent wide use of Dr. Johnson's Dictionary.

Realizing that there were in any case not enough roman letters to go round, he set himself firmly against any attempt at rearrangement of those letters (this is what *he* called 'spelling reform'), and he had additional reasons for so doing: the impression of near-illiteracy that he claimed was made on educated people by rearranged, 'phonetic' spellings, and the likelihood that such spellings might have undesirable, possibly obscene, associations.

Towards the end of his life this campaign seems to have been intensified, in long letters to *The Times* newspaper and elsewhere, since he had formed the idea of leaving his fortune to promote a new alphabet; but many years before, in his Preface to *Pygmalion*—a play whose principal theme was the *pronunciation* of English—we find him alluding to English in its written form. I quote: 'The English have no respect for their language, and will not teach their children to speak it. They cannot write it, because they have nothing to write it with but an old foreign alphabet of which only the consonants, and not all of them, have any agreed speech value'.

I mentioned a moment ago that Shaw always wrote his works using Pitman's Shorthand (his secretary then transcribed this into longhand for revision, and the printer). It might perhaps be thought that here surely was the answer to Shaw's quest for a new script for English, in other words that a system of shorthand (not necessarily Pitman's) would achieve the economy—at least of time—that was wanted. But this is far from being the case. In the first place, the all-purpose utility of an orthography cannot be achieved by any system of writing based upon hand movements and designed with considerations of sheer speed primarily— almost exclusively—in mind. Technical problems arising for the printer would alone rule out sequences of shorthand strokes where individual letters have no separate identity.

It is notable that existing scripts based on a cursive style, such as Arabic, lend themselves extremely awkwardly to handling by the modern technologies of printing and typing, designed for handling separate, discrete letter shapes. Because the majority of Arabic letters *have* to be joined to a following one in the same word (a few may *not* be so joined), the typewriter and printing press are required to simulate this joining up of successive letters, by bringing the final stroke of one letter and the beginning stroke of the following one extremely close together, so that they appear to touch. And because no overlapping of forms can be obtained from mechanical devices that move forward a notch at a time for a letter of whatever shape to be placed in the given space, awkward distortions of letters are unavoidable, and there is a wastefully high proportion of white space to black letter on the printed page, particularly since the large number of essential diacritical dots above and below each line of writing makes it necessary to set successive lines a considerable distance apart in the interests of legibility. Shorthand too is notoriously wasteful of space, the spidery outlines having a vertical as well as a horizontal sprawl. Yet further objections to a shorthand can be made: that it tends to become illegible to all save the writer, and even to him or (more often) her after any lapse of time before the eventual intended retranscription into longhand; that the sought-after speed itself is not attained without such drastic abbreviations and omissions that ambiguities constantly arise or illegibility even results.

Shaw himself realized the fundamental unsuitability of a shorthand as an orthography, though he did on one occasion (Preface to *The Miraculous Birth of Language* by R. A. Wilson) hold up, as a model of what could be done, Henry Sweet's Current Shorthand. He went on to point out that the basic strokes devised by Sweet would have suited very well, if only Sweet had not himself gone on to complicate and bedevil matters by seeking to make his system suitable for verbatim reporting, with its inevitable contractions and innumerable conventions. (It is, however, interesting to realize that it was Shaw's racy description of Sweet's Current

Shorthand contained in the above Preface—"A straight line, written with a single stroke of the pen, can represent four different consonants by varying its length and position. Put a hook at the top of it, and you have four more consonants. Put a hook at the lower end, and . . . etc."—that provided the inspiration for the designer of what was eventually to become the "Shavian" of today, as it may well have done also for many of the other competitors in the Bernard Shaw Alphabet Competition. But I anticipate.)

The events following upon Shaw's death in 1950 must be fairly well known to Shaw-lovers and spelling reformers alike, so I think I need only summarize them here, and recall how Shaw, in his Will, appointed the Public Trustee to be his executor and trustee, and imposed on him the duty of seeking and publishing an alphabet of at least forty letters, more efficient than the existing one of twenty-six letters, so as to enable 'the said language (English) to be written without indicating single sounds by groups of letters or by diacritical marks'; this alphabet he termed 'Proposed British Alphabet'; how Shaw's residuary estate was directed by him to be held for a period in certain trusts for this purpose, but this was declared by a Judge of the High Court to be invalid in law. The Public Trustee appealed from the decision, and by way of compromise the residuary legatees (the British Museum, the Royal Academy of Dramatic Art, and the National Gallery of Ireland) eventually agreed to pay a certain sum to the Public Trustee for the promotion of this project of a new alphabet. It was indeed a modest sum in relation to Shaw's estate as a whole at that time, and much more so since that estate began to be augmented by the massive royalties that have been coming in since the appearance of *My Fair Lady*. However, it was the best that could be managed—and it has been instrumental in the creation of Shavian. Not until 1957 were all the legal complications out of the way, and the field cleared for the Public Trustee to inaugurate the Alphabet Competition by offering a prize of £500 for the best design of a new alphabet complying with the provisions of Shaw's Will.

109

Technical advice was available to the Public Trustee from a panel of three outside specialists, who also acted as judges for the Competition. As one of those judges I had the interesting experience of examining each of the 467 entries that came in during 1958. By the end of the following year the work of judging was completed, and the Public Trustee announced that the prize money would be divided equally between four competitors, none of whom had submitted a design outstanding enough to be accepted as it stood, i.e. to be the 'Proposed British Alphabet', for use in the subsequent transliteration of Shaw's play *Androcles and the Lion*, as stipulated in his Will.

Now, clearly, that transliteration could not possibly be made until there was an alphabet to transliterate into. So a problem still remained. This the Public Trustee sought to resolve by inviting the four prizewinners to work further on their designs with a view to arriving at the best possible solution. This did not mean (as on the surface might have appeared to be the case) that the best features of each entrant's work could be extracted and somehow fused into the ideal alphabet: a glance at the individual entries would be sufficient to make it plain that the basic conceptions of each were so utterly different that a combination of any features drawn from more than one of them could only have created a hotch-potch that would have been unsatisfactory from practically every point of view, could not possibly have produced an aesthetically pleasing and harmonious whole, and would have been almost certainly inferior to each of the prizewinning entries considered separately. What in fact happened was that each of the prizewinners was encouraged to do further work on his submitted design in the light of criticism and comments by the judges. I was asked to conduct any ensuing correspondence, and to begin by letting each entrant know what we thought in detail of his entry. Now we, in the course of our judging, had had the opportunity (and, I must say for myself, the extremely interesting experience) not only of inspecting several hundred newly-designed original alphabets, but of forming each his own

110

opinion, and our joint opinions, based on the experience so gained as to the basic criteria for a script suitable for the transliteration—the minimum requirements, as it were, that any proposed alphabet should conform to for complete acceptability. Just because no individual competitor had met all these demands, the prize-money had not been awarded to one outstandingly successful design.

The response of the four competitors was varied; one dropped out immediately and took no further part in the proceedings; one submitted several completely fresh designs in a short space of time; one entered into very full discussion with me, in the light of which he set about modifying his design. This last was Mr. Kingsley Read, whose final re-cast version was eventually re-submitted to all the judges and approved for use in the transliteration, thus becoming 'Shavian', the Bernard Shaw Alphabet. The extent of the re-casting may be judged from the fact that only about ten characters out of the total of 48 reappeared unchanged, and of these not more than two or three retain their original value, i.e. stand for the sound they stood for previously. Yet the overall appearance of the design is so similar as to be un-mistakably the work of the same hand, and quite unlike all other entries. It may be of interest if I mention the main feature in Mr. Read's competition entry that the judges considered unsatisfactory and that he later eliminated success-fully: it was that certain letter shapes were used unchanged for different sounds except for being placed in different positions in relation to other letters; for instance a given shape might be placed high in relation to the line of writing to stand for one sound, and the same shape placed low in relation to the line to stand for some other sound. This would mean, of course, that the form itself could never be interpreted unambiguously in isolation, i.e. without other letters or at least some essential guide line or rule from which to judge its relative position. When this disadvantage was brought to the designer's attention, he found himself in-volved in the radical re-casting described above, but even-tually came up with the masterly solution we see today.

111

In executing the transliteration, I had a number of decisions of my own to make, notably as to the treatment of the letter R, the representation of syllabic consonants, of strong and weak forms, and of course the spelling of a number of doubtful words. This included the problem of many words having acceptable alternative pronunciations, even without going outside the general type of English that Shaw himself had stipulated, namely that spoken by His Majesty King George V. This the judges were able to interpret as indicating a pronunciation widely known to linguists and phoneticians as RP. I decided too that though Americans might favour a certain number of spelling differences, to fit better their own *distribution* of sounds (their, or anyone's, different manner of *pronouncing* English sounds as such being irrelevant to the orthography), nevertheless the proper way to transcribe this, the first publication in Shavian, emanating from Britain and moreover conforming to Shaw's prescription, was to transliterate the words in accordance with the conventions of the new system and in line generally with the pronunciations likely to be heard on the English stage.

Here now is a specimen of Shavian printing—the second part of the Gettysburg Address by Abraham Lincoln. There follow reproductions of the two sides of the card inserted in each copy of *Androcles and the Lion*, Shaw Alphabet Edition, (Penguin Books Ltd.), on which appear classified lists of the Shavian letters, with keywords that serve also as the actual names of those letters, by the help of which the connected text may be deciphered. Alternatively, the New Spelling version of the Address (p. 118) may be consulted for this purpose.

Let me draw your attention to some of the salient features of the script.

Shavian is written, and read, from left to right across the page or other writing surface, in lines which run from top to bottom of the page—just as they do in current roman usage. There is of course nothing inevitable or universal about our present way of doing these things,—and a certain number of the competition entries did propose a departure from tradition in this very matter; nevertheless the winning entry un-doubtedly commended itself to the judges on the grounds (among many others) that in it, established practice as to the direction of the writing was to be retained.

A line of writing consists of a sequence of separate letter shapes (apart from ligatured forms, see below), and these are grouped by words, i.e. with a blank space to mark off word division. In this respect too, as also in matters of punctu-ation generally, current usage remains unaltered.

Letters are of three sizes in the vertical dimension:— Shorts, corresponding to lower-case sorts of x—or ribbon—height; Talls, that ascend above the ribbon while standing on the same base; and Deeps, that fall from the top level of the ribbon to below its base. In other words, here again there is little departure from the present state of affairs in printed roman (some *cursive* roman forms, e.g. handwritten *f*, may both ascend and descend from the ribbon). The proportion of ascenders and descenders to x-height letters has been arranged to be about the same as in roman, but ascenders and descenders are more equally distributed than now as between one another (there being in roman about six times as many ascending letters as descending letters on the printed page). These changes have been intentionally introduced in the knowledge that in normal rapid reading, words are recognized as wholes, and that it is visible differ-ences in the external outline or silhouette of words that are mainly instrumental in enabling the eye rapidly to dis-criminate between different words and so to grasp their meaning. Long sequences of x-height letters tend of course towards uniformity of both top and bottom outline, but sequences of letters standing on the base of the ribbon, i.e. those of x-height together with those having ascenders, (which would produce uniformity of the bottom outline) are as a result of this alteration less likely to occur in Shavian than in roman. It may however be noted that the Shavian Talls and Deeps do not depend for identification solely on the fact of their having ascenders and descenders respectively: they are already adequately differentiated by their intrinsic shapes. So it would be perfectly feasible, and might well be found desirable for certain purposes, e.g. display work, to use founts of letters all of one size—there being in any case no capitals.

This brings me to the first point to be mentioned thus far, embodying a notable divergence from current roman usage (aside, that is, from the forms and general appearance of the Shavian letters themselves); there is to be no difference of shape (or size or thickness, though these would be optional) between initial and other letters, thus eliminating one of the major objections to current roman usage: the fact that the 26 letters have so many alternative shapes—for capitals and lower-case, not to mention cursive forms. To meet the occasional need for an equivalent to capitalization, a raised 'namer' dot is available in Shavian, e.g. for proper names, at least at their first occurrence in a text, or where obscurity might otherwise result.

As regards handwritten Shavian, the letters have deliberately been designed so as to discourage the cursive writing of linking strokes not forming part of a letter, thus eliminating a source of much ambiguity and illegibility in connected writing. If adjacent letters lend themselves to joining without extra linking strokes, they may well be joined (as the printed Shavian ligatures are joined), but not otherwise, the inevitable upward movements of the hand between letters being made off the writing surface (i.e. in the air) instead of in contact with it, with, it is believed, little if any overall slowing down of hand movements, once the somewhat different technique of writing has been acquired. Moreover much thought was devoted to ensuring that the actual shapes chosen for letters should, in the interest of legibility, not lend themselves to confusion with one another when written at speed, or to distortion from their basic shape, leading in the long run to divergences arising between printed (or typed) and handwritten forms—which is of course what has happened in roman, thus giving rise to the multiplicity of forms referred to above. Even supposing it were found in practice (and this is by no means proved) that writers tended

114

by the nature of the script to form slightly more deliberate strokes, this would be very much to the advantage of the Shavian *reader* in ease of deciphering.

In fact, of course, overall writing time for the equivalent text would be reduced (given comparable familiarity with the script and its writing technique) on a number of counts: firstly, the 'silent' letters of present roman would naturally not be written at all—about one letter in six is now redundant; secondly, fewer strokes per letter are used in Shavian, so more letters can be written in a given time, or at the maximum speed at which an individual hand can form successive strokes. It may be noticed how simple are the actual shapes of the letters, a high proportion consisting of just a single stroke, and only one requiring as many as two down-strokes and more than one abrupt change of direction of pen on paper. Thirdly, much attention has been given to the allocation of the simplest available shapes to the most frequently occurring sounds. Fourthly, single-letter abbreviation for the four commonest English words (the, of, and, to) are standard Shavian—and a number of other word-signs or reduced forms may well be used besides.

Eight of the printer's shorts shown in Specimen 2 are in fact compounds, i.e. ligatures, six of these being vowel + *r* in some commonly occurring cases, including one vowel that is itself already made up of a combination of two others. These compounds are to be written whether or not they be indicative of an individual writer's or speaker's use of *r* as distributed in his natural speech, thus enabling the Shavian spellings used by Londoners, Scots, Americans, etc., to resemble one another in respect of *r*—as they do in the standard orthography today. As to whether *any* alternative spellings would be available to speakers of different kinds of English (involving different distribution of their sounds), the answer is that they would, but I will not here attempt to go into details, and will only say that it would clearly be in the interest of a new world orthography for English that variation between writer and writer should be kept to a minimum. The two remaining compound sorts are ligatures of two other juxtaposed letters, which, as with the vowel + *r* ligatures, may be looked upon as instances in print of the permissible easy linking of handwritten forms referred to above. However, on the Shavian typewriter keyboard (which is now available to the public) these ligatured forms are not found each on their own key, but are to be typed with the separate keys for the two letters concerned. This is partly to economize keys, but also because a closer approximation to equal width of all letters, on the equal-space typewriter, gives a better appearance to the page of typescript than would otherwise be the case. Copies of *Shaw-Script*, the quarterly periodical entirely produced in Shavian, from the Shavian typewriter keyboard, may be inspected in order to judge the effect.

Further study of the Shavian alphabet and of the relationship of letters to the sounds they stand for will make it plain that this is a coherent system, on a carefully considered plan embodying many distinct (and sometimes mutually conflicting) points, which has at times been obliged by the nature of the case to compromise, though without, I believe, abandoning any important theoretical principle or upsetting the harmonious working or appearance of the whole. It will become apparent that there are in the letter shapes many visual parallels to the phonetic or other relationships between sounds: thus, for instance, all vowels are Shorts; sixteen consonants are paired on a voiced|voiceless basis where this contrast functions within the language, the voiced Deep letter being the turned counterpart of the voiceless Tall in each case; the four other pairs, similarly related visually, record other types of relationship.

In conclusion, I do not feel it incumbent upon me to enlarge upon the conjectural future of Shavian: my interest in it has been largely professional, but this interest is still very much alive. At this moment I am concerned with the statistical estimate, stipulated in Shaw's Will, of the number of people writing English in the world today, on which it is intended to base an estimate of the economic savings to be achieved by its use. When this work has been completed, and

116

perhaps some report on it made public, the last wishes of the late George Bernard Shaw will have been fully carried out. Whether or not the Shavian alphabet becomes more widely known or eventually adopted (or something like it) depends on its intrinsic merits and on the extent to which the purpose it is intended to serve kindles a spark in the minds of the present or of some future generation.

# Index